THE RELATIONAL IMPERATIVE

Resources for a World on Edge

Kenneth J. Gergen

Taos Institute Publications
Chagrin Falls, Ohio
USA

The Relational Imperative
Resources for a World on Edge

Taos Institute Publications
A Division of the Taos Institute
Chagrin Falls, Ohio
USA

ISBN-13: 978-1-938552-85-4 (paperback)
ISBN-13: 978-1-938552-90-8 (ebook)

LCCN: 2021948550

Taos Institute Publications

The Taos Institute is a nonprofit organization dedicated to the development of social constructionist theory and practice for purposes of world benefit. Constructionist theory and practice locate the source of meaning, value, and action in communicative relations among people. Our major investment is in fostering relational processes that can enhance the welfare of people and the world in which they live. Taos Institute Publications offers contributions to cutting-edge theory and practice in social construction. Our books are designed for scholars, practitioners, students, and the openly curious public. The **Children's Books Series** is our newest series of books related to social construction and positive change in the world. The **Focus Book Series** provides brief introductions and overviews that illuminate theories, concepts, and useful practices. The **Tempo Book Series** is especially dedicated to the general public and to practitioners. The **Books for Professionals Series** provides in-depth works that focus on recent developments in theory and practice. **WorldShare Books** is an online offering of books in PDF format for free download from our website. Our books are particularly relevant to social scientists and to practitioners concerned with individual, family, organizational, community, and societal change.

— Kenneth J. Gergen
President, Board of Directors
The Taos Institute

Taos Institute Board of Directors

Harlene Anderson
Kristin Bodiford
Duane Bidwell
Celiane Camargo Borges
Kenneth J. Gergen
David Cooperrider, Honorary

Paloma Torres Dávila
Sally St. George
Sheila McNamee
Monica Sesma
Dan Wulff
Diana Whitney, Emerita

WorldShare Books Editor – Dan Wulff
Books for Professional Series Editor – Kenneth Gergen
Tempo Series Editor – Duane Bidwell
Focus Book Series Editor – Harlene Anderson
Executive Director – Dawn Dole

For information about the Taos Institute and social constructionism visit:
www.taosinstitute.net

Dedicated to

Mary M. Gergen

1938-2020

Beloved Companion and Relational Inspirator

Contents

Preface... vii

1. Entering the Relational World.......................................1

2. Living in the Relational Flow 21

3. Education as Relational Process 43

4. Healthcare: From Causality to Collaboration 65

5. Organizations and the Challenge of Change.............................85

6. Conflict, Control, and the Relational Imperative......................109

Preface

LET ME SHARE SOME OF my concerns in writing this book:

- The world is in a state of increasingly rapid and unpredictable change. There seems little that we can hold on to, little that is solid or reliable.

- With a world in flux, our institutions are no longer adequate. Education seems increasingly irrelevant; organizations can't be managed; governments can't be trusted.

- Everywhere there is antagonism – among religions, political parties, nations, racial and ethnic groups, economic classes, and more. Conflicts are becoming increasingly deadly.

- There seems little in the way of moral compass. Multiple values, ideologies, and beliefs leave us either fighting with each other or condemned as relativists.

- The world's nations are primarily interested in their own wellbeing, while threats to global wellbeing – such as climate change, deadly viruses, and injustice – are sacrificed. Collective action is an afterthought.

If such concerns are also yours, you should find this book an engaging companion. These are indeed daunting challenges, but my hope is that by walking together – author and reader – we may create promising paths forward.

My central offering for this journey is a fresh perspective. In grappling with these enormous challenges, we primarily base our deliberations on the idea that the world is made up of independent, or bounded units. The units can be individual persons, for example, or families, schools, organizations, governments, and so on. On this account, relationships are secondary, resulting from the interaction between two or more units. The present offering makes a radical leap: It is the relational process that is primary, and it is within that process that units acquire their identity. From this process our educational systems emerge, health and illness take shape, and organizations and nations thrive or perish. If we are to make headway in dealing with the challenges ahead, attention to this process is imperative. The future of planetary life depends on its well-being. In attending to single notes, harmony remains elusive.

Many of the central ideas in this book were developed in an earlier and more extended work, *Relational Being: Beyond Self and Community*. Many readers found the proposals both challenging and inspiring. My plan for the present book was thus to offer a brief but accessible vehicle for sharing these earlier ideas. However, the world has changed since the 2009 publication of the original work. Two major movements are noteworthy, as they have significantly altered the course of the present writing. The first is the increasing sense of a world out of control. We realize that the digital revolution has unleashed an unprecedented wave of challenges and opportunities.

In the blink of an eye, any local event, initiative, image, or opinion may leap to the global stage, with multiple and unpredictable consequences. At the same time, we witness the continuous degrading of the environment. Vanishing water supplies, rampant forest fires, and devastating hurricanes, bring global warming into stark visibility. And while the 2020 Covid 19 pandemic makes it painfully clear that "we are all in this together," we lack the capacities for uniting.

A second major movement offers hope. This movement grows from the increased concerns with precisely the problems, potentials and practices of relating. Emerging from around the world is a dazzling array of relationally sensitive innovations. New and promising practices spring to life – in education, therapy, health care, organization development, governance, and more. One senses a swelling consciousness that we *can* find ways of successfully going on together. My hope in the present book is that a relational perspective can bring unity and strength to this movement, and the resources can inspire the continuing development of more viable and flourishing futures.

– Kenneth J. Gergen

1. Entering the Relational World

The limits of our language are
the limits of our world.

– Ludwig Wittgenstein

THE CREATIVE CAPACITIES OF HUMAN beings are enormous. Even within the past century we have harnessed atomic energy, flown to the moon, and developed technologies for communicating instantaneously around the globe. Strangely, however, when we turn to our relations with each other, we find little to match such achievements. Despite thousands of years of living together, daily life is marked by distrust, prejudice, callousness, and selfishness. On a larger scale, we continue to confront polarized conflict, injustice, oppression, and bloodshed. Why have we failed so badly in our human efforts to make progress in our ways of relating? Is it possible that we have been blinded by our assumptions, our ways of deliberating, and our commonsense ways of going on together? Perhaps the very language we use in our deliberations stands in our way.

This is no small matter, as the global challenges become ever more threatening. With the emergence of globe-spanning technologies, every local problem is potentially global, all traditions may antagonize others, and new movements may burst forth at any moment. As it is said, we now confront "wicked problems," that is, problems of urgent importance but so complex, ever changing, and requiring so much information, that they defy solution. The present work breaks with the traditional tools of understanding, and opens the door to a radical departure in comprehending ourselves, our world, and our ways of living together.

To appreciate the potential, consider the common presumption that the social world is made up of separate persons. We thus focus carefully on the qualities and characteristics of the individuals. We have thousands of terms for talking about an individual's mental states – emotions, thoughts, memories, moods, values, and so on. These are the tools we use in making decisions about our lives and our future. And when things go wrong in our relationships, we thus begin to ask, who is responsible? Which individual is at fault? This same focus on the independent units also fills our discussions of families, schools, organizations, and nations. We focus on the quality of family life, the character of the local school, the make-up of the police department, and so on. In the case of nations, we have libraries filled with accounts of individual nations, their origins, histories, and characteristics. Essentially, our vocabulary of understanding is dominated by a *presumption of separation*. As a result, our vocabulary for talking about the relations among the separate entities is impoverished. It's as if we have thousands of terms for describing individual chess pieces but little to say about the game. For champions at chess, the reverse is true.

So, this book is about suspending the focus on bounded units, and exploring the processes of relating. In the present chapter we first take a closer look at the assumption of separation. Of particular concern are its corrosive consequences for our lives. This will prepare the way for a change in paradigms: from a world of separation to a world of *relational processes*.[1] As we shall explore, virtually all our actions – including our views of what is real, rational, and right – owe their existence to this process. Indeed, it is from this process that emerge what we take to be the qualities and characteristics of the participants. In Chapter 2 a focus on relational process in daily life will advance an understanding of a relational perspective. While these opening chapters focus on daily relations, we then move to realms of more sweeping consequence. Here we explore applications in education, therapy and medical care, organizational life, conflict, and governance. In each case we find invaluable innovations for going on together in a world on edge.

Beyond Individual and the Community

If you were asked to describe the world around you at this moment, what would you say? Perhaps you would talk about various objects – a desk, a computer, a lamp, a chair, and so on. And there is a window, a door, and perhaps a friend seated across the room. Life as usual… But let's take a closer look at what is assumed in this simple description. What you have supplied is a kind of inventory of independent objects or entities. Here is a table, there a chair, and over there a friend, and so on. One might say it is a world made up of *independent*

---

1. The term "relational" can be used in many ways, not all of which are congenial. The present account is radical in many respects, and may possibly be distinguished from others in its designation as relational process theory.

units. For most of these units we have rich vocabularies of description. Consider, for example, all that you might have to say about the computer, or your friend. Understanding the world in terms of units is not a new idea. In Western culture it can be traced to the writings of the early Greek philosopher Democritus. Democritus proposed that our world is basically composed of physically indivisible units called atoms. Such a view is still with us; atomic physics is only one example. Most important, this atomistic worldview is now the world of common sense – a world of desks, computers, and friends.

To be sure, this atomized view of the world has its uses. Not only do most of our activities in daily life depend on it, but much of science as well. Of particular interest, however, is the way we come to understand ourselves – as independent individuals. We are each identified by names (along with a host of numbers and passwords) designed to differentiate us from others. This way of understanding ourselves – as separated or bounded units – is also tied to shared values and ways of life. In much of the world, personal freedom and autonomy are cherished; individual achievements and acts of heroism are prized; individual laziness and cowardice are maligned. Not only do these values shape daily life, but they are also built into many of our institutions. In schools, for example, we evaluate individual students; each is held responsible for doing independent work. In the workplace, we hire individual workers, evaluate their individual performance, and eliminate those whose work is inferior. In courts of law we decide on the guilt or innocence of individuals. The institution of Western democracy is similarly based on the value of individual choice, and the right to self-determination.

So, What's the Problem?

If we live comfortably within the tradition of independent selves, why should we seek an alternative? Here it is essential to realize that an atomized view of the world is only one way of understanding. You may see yourself as separate from others, but in most circles you are simply "them." That we believe we are independent individuals – each possessing our very own thoughts, feelings, and desires – is a child of history and culture. As noted anthropologist Clifford Geertz remarked:

> The Western conception of the person as a bounded, unique,... dynamic center of awareness, emotion, judgment, and action organized into a distinctive whole and set against other such wholes ...is a rather peculiar idea within the context of the world's cultures.[2]

If we can recognize that the way we understand ourselves and the world, and the values we place on these understandings are not required by the way the world is, then we are free to ask about the limits or shortcomings of where we stand. And, if we do find problems, we can explore and create alternatives. In this light, let's consider a few of the most prominent critiques of the individualist tradition:

Me first! If we are fundamentally independent of each other – and I am responsible for my actions – then what is the aim of life? One obvious answer to this question is to take care of myself. Make sure **I** am ok – safe, nourished, and successful. This is also the view of countless social scientists. As Sigmund Freud proposed, we are

---

2. Geertz, C . (1979) *From the native's point of view: On the nature of anthropological understanding.* In P. Rabinow and W.M. Sullivan (Eds) Interpretive social science. Berkeley, CA: University of California Press. p. 59

born with a fundamental desire for self-pleasure.[3] The humanist psychologist Abraham Maslow proposed that the highest human need is for *self*-actualization.[4] Contemporary economists base their theories of economic behavior on the individual's fundamental desire to maximize self-gain and minimize loss. Socio-biologists argue that the human's basic motive is to further one's own genes.[5] All of these ideas support the rationale for putting ourselves first. There are other names for this: selfishness, egotism, narcissism...

The me-first orientation is also related to issues of ethics and trust, In the case of ethics, there is a longstanding emphasis in Western ethics on care for the other. Exemplary is the Christian injunction, "You shall love your neighbor as yourself." It is just such values that undergird traditions of charity and philanthropy. Yet, while we may prize such efforts it is important to realize that they too sustain the presumption of separation: "you" should love "your neighbor" "as yourself" – ah, your first love. If we understand that love of self is primary, we also establish the grounds for suspicion of others. No one can be fully trusted beyond what they gain for themselves. This includes family members, neighbors, merchants, politicians, and beyond. Even vows of love may mask the possibility that you are just a "good deal." It's only smart, as they say, to "Look out for number one."

I am better than you...or am I? Given the focus on *myself,* it is obvious to ask, "How do I compare with others...am I superior...am I inferior?" These become a central issue in social life. This process of *social comparison*, as psychologists call it, has two unfortunate

---

3. Freud, S. (1933) *New Introductory lectures on psycho-analysis*. London: Hogarth.
4. Maslow, A. (1987) *Motivation and personality*. New York: Knapp. 3rd ed.
5. Dawkins, R. (1976) *The selfish gene*. London: Oxford University Press.

consequences. The first is the problem of self-esteem. When others seem "better than me," or when "I am second rate," the result is typically a sense of self-doubt or insecurity. Therapists have long noted the pervasive need for self-esteem in Western culture. People doubt their worth, their abilities, their likability, their appearance, and so on. From psychotherapy to educational programs designed to boost student self-esteem, the attempt is to help people feel *ok*. Then there is the mushrooming of health clubs, plastic surgery, the fashion industry, and the multi-billion-dollar cosmetics industry that all feed on the insecurity that in some way, one may be lacking. Importantly, if we didn't embrace the assumption of separation, the problem of self-esteem would wither away.

The second unfortunate consequence of social comparison is the seeking of superiority – to be better than others. Wherever there are comparisons of better or worse, there is an invitation to be better. This may mean finding reasons to justify one's superiority – to rationalize why one's morality, culture, religion, or aesthetic tastes, for example, are "the best." In the same way, students who make high grades in school may look down on those who score lower; those with more wealth than others may see themselves as better, more deserving, or more hard-working; as commonly put, "no one likes a loser. Here you can also see that the stage is set for social division and conflict.

Why should I bother? If we live in a world of fundamentally separated individuals, then relationships are secondary. They only exist when two or more individuals come together. They are artificial contrivances that we can "build," or "work on, and abandon if they don't fulfill our needs. We feel justified in leaving a relationship if it constrains our freedom or undermines our personal growth. We are also encouraged to ask, "How much am I getting from this relationship?" "How much is it costing me in time and effort?" As social scientists put it, we acquire an *instrumental attitude* toward others. We begin to treat others as mere instruments for fulfilling our own needs and desires? And if they are not fulfilled – if the costs are more than the gains – then isn't it time to "go my own way?" What's the point of remaining in a marriage, one might ask, "when it's no fun for me," or going to family events "when I get nothing from it," or doing political work just to help the community? Don't I have to "look out for myself first?"

Selfishness, distrust, anxiety, jealousy, alienation, destructive impulses, and social irresponsibility – these are only a few of the outcomes of the common belief in independent selves. There are others. Critics of the individualist tradition have also located sources for racism, greed, economic exploitation, and the common indifference to poverty.[6] There is ample reason to reconsider.

Is Community a Solution?

If our traditions of understanding are harmful to our lives together, how can we escape "common sense"? And even if we could, are there alternatives? The most obvious answer is to search for other traditions, and learn from their ways of life. Contrasted with Western individualist culture, there are many cultures of the world in which the single individual is not at the center of the stage. Most visible among these alternatives are what are often called *communal* societies. It is not the individual who is prized, but the group to which the individual belongs. The group could be a family, a community, a

---

6. See additional readings at the end of the chapter.

tribe, a caste, a religion, a nation, and so on, but one's individual life is secondary to the well-being of the whole. For many of the world's peoples this communal way of life has brought security, direction, moral clarity, trust, and meaning.

However, as widely recognized, a communally centered life also has significant shortcomings. Allegiance to the group can be stifling. New ideas, alternative perspectives, and creative expressions may threaten the group tradition or doctrine. Deviating from religious or political authority, for example, can lead to imprisonment or execution. There are also problems in making intelligent decisions. When a high priority is placed on group agreement, there is little place for the deviant thinker. The term *groupthink* refers to cases in which the demand for group solidarity leads to narrow, insensitive and simplistic decisions. And, in a world where technology creates conditions of rapid and unpredictable change, restricting deliberation to the group voice is a recipe for disaster.

More generally, however, the celebration of the group carries with it many of the same problems as a commitment to individual selves. Both the individual and the group are essentially *independent entities*. This means that many of the problems we encountered in the case of individualism, are echoed on a group level. As we devote ourselves to "our group first;" other groups become invisible, alien, or dangerous. It's "us vs. them." In the competition between political parties the nation suffers; in the competition among nations global well-being suffers. If "our group" is superior, we have the right to rule. *We* become the owners of the Truth, a nation above all, a people singled out by God, a master race, and so on. Here lie the seeds of sweeping brutality.

Toward a Relational Alternative

In the beginning is the relationship.
– Martin Buber

We are now at a critical turning point in the discussion. We have scanned two highly revered traditions of understanding who we are as human beings. Both are based on the idea of bounded entities: the autonomous individual on the one hand and the primacy of the group on the other. Both traditions have contributed much to our valued ways of life, but simultaneously at the cost of substantial suffering. The present question – challenging and profound – is how we can understand our social world in any other way? How can we hammer out an understanding that might avoid the pitfalls of fundamental separation and self-seeking? More importantly, could such an alternative open the way to more viable and flourishing ways of life?

Co-Action: The Relational Origins of Meaning

Seeing the shortcomings of the individualist tradition, many thinkers have turned to the importance of relationships in our lives. They have variously emphasized the importance of loving one another, compassion, generosity, tolerance, respect, moral responsibility, and so on. However, most of these attempts begin with the assumption of bounded beings, and how they should ideally treat each other. In effect, the individual remains the primary entity, fundamentally separated, but is then invited, reminded, and begged to care for the other. What if we reverse the order of significance, and begin with *relational process*, a condition of fundamental union? In this case, whatever may be said of individuals may emerge from the forms of relating.

Let us begin with a visual illustration. Consider the ways you might organize three random lines on a piece of paper. For example, here they are arranged to form what we commonly take to be an arrow, the English letter H, and an ominous face.

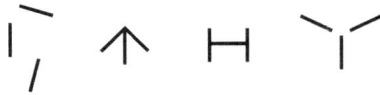

$$\begin{array}{cccc} \overline{} & & & \overline{} \\ \big|_{\displaystyle /} & \uparrow & \mathsf{H} & \mathsf{Y} \end{array}$$

The lines are without significance in themselves, independent of each other. However, when they are related in these various ways they become meaning/full. Using the same logic, consider the following individual words: *is, dress, a, really, that, pretty*. Each word by itself – without any context – is as meaningless as a random line. It is when we place them into a particular relationship that they become meaningful: *That is really a pretty dress.* But now let's put these words into action. Imagine they are spoken by a man strolling down the street and randomly addressing them to anyone passing by. Chances are you would wonder if he were mentally ill, someone to be avoided. Standing alone, the utterance is ambiguous – much like the unrelated lines in the visual illustration. In contrast, then, let's say the man – call him Rolf – spoke these words to Sandra, a colleague in his workplace when she passes him in the hall. In this context the words begin to acquire meaning, possibly as a nice compliment.

But let's imagine that Sandra was preoccupied with a presentation she was preparing, and didn't hear Rolf's words. Could we then call the utterance a compliment? The words may sound like a compliment, but until coordinated in some way with Sandra's acknowledgment, the sounds are merely floating in space. So, let's say that Sandra looks up from her paper and responds with, "Oh, thank you!"

With Sandra's reply, the utterance now becomes meaningful as a compliment. Metaphorically, in her act of appreciation Sandra gives birth to the Rolf's words as a compliment.

This may seem straightforward enough, but now consider Sandra's utterance, "Oh, thank you!" While this appears to be an act of appreciation, what if she were strolling down the street randomly uttering these words to no one in particular? This would be puzzling, possibly an indication of madness. Her utterance was not, then, an act of appreciation *in itself*. It only became so when coordinated with Rolf's particular comment to her. Echoing the above, Rolf's comment to her planted the seed from which she could give it birth as a compliment.

As we see, neither the "compliment" nor the "appreciation" exists as an individual's independent action. The actions only become recognized as meaningful *in their relation to each other*. In effect, Rolf and Sandra require each other to have meaning at all. More formally we might say, through *coordinated action*, or *co-action*, the two of them come into meaning. Without coordination, their words lapse into nonsense. Coordination precedes content. And so it is with all the words in our possession. No single individual created a word. Our sounds only become *words* through coordinated action. Or as Wittgenstein proposed, there is no "private language,"—known only to a lone individual. It is only within the process of coordination that utterances become language.[7] When we speak to another, we thus draw from a history of coordination – sometimes ancient in origin. But in the moment we speak, we hang on the edge of nonsense. Our lives as meaningful beings will be restored (or not) in what follows.

---

7. Wittgenstein, L. (1978) *Philosophical investigations*. Oxford: Blackwell. (243)

Meaning in Motion

If we observe two people in dialogue, we typically focus our attention on whoever is speaking. It is thus that in the movies, we see the screen first filled with the face of the actress expressing herself to the actor, and the camera then pans to the actor as he responds. But in this depiction, we are scarcely conscious of the most crucial element: *the coordination of their expressions*. It is only within the coordination that the utterances become sensible at all. To further appreciate the significance of the coordination, let's return to Rolf's complement. What if Sandra had responded to his utterances in the following ways:

Rolf: *That is really a pretty dress.*

Sandra: *Say that one more time, and I will report you for harassment!*

   or

Rolf: *That is really a pretty dress.*

Sandra: *That's so sweet of you. Come and have a coffee with me.*

In the first example, what had seemed a compliment now becomes an inappropriate advance; in the second, the same words are now given birth as a romantic invitation. In effect, Rolf is not in control of the meaning of his words. At that moment, his future depends on her reply.

It is interesting here to consider our concern with the character or personality of those about us. *What is he or she like as a person?* We may describe this person as *warm*, and another as *cold,* this one as *generous* and another as *stingy*. And as we sometimes ask ourselves:

"Am I…" *smart…self-centered…creative…idealistic…timid*? All such questions treat the characteristics as inhering in the individual person. As in the case of chess, the focus is on the individual chess piece. But now, return to the previous examples. Is Rolf a team builder who gives compliments, a male predator, a sweet romantic, or…? His words are identical in each case, but our sense of his character takes shape through his colleague's response. In the same way, none of us are smart, self-centered, or creative independent of others. There are no comedians without those who laugh. We are not the owners of what we mean or who we are. It is within the relational process that we find ourselves, lose ourselves, and are reborn.

Yet, our focus is still too narrow. We extracted but a single pair of coordinated utterances from the ongoing flow of life. While we left Sandra with the last word in defining her colleague, the process of meaning making is ongoing. Her words now stand open to Rolf's reply. Consider the following possibilities:

Rolf: *That is really a pretty dress.*

Sandra: *Say that one more time, and I will report you for harassment!*

Rolf: *It's really a pity you don't know a compliment when you see one.*

Rolf: *That is really a pretty dress.*

Sandra: *Say that one more time, and I will report you for harassment!*

Rolf: *Everyone says you are paranoid, and now I believe it!*

In his reply to Sandra, Rolf has now defined her character – possibly as insensitive in the first case and mentally disturbed in the second. And in refashioning her character in these ways, we cannot easily conclude that he is a male predator. But, as you can see, Rolf does not have the last word on this matter. As the conversation continues, with each remark giving shape to what has preceded, so the participants' characters may evolve. In the same way, schools create failing students, psychiatrists create the mentally ill, and courts of law create criminals. But should these institutions have "the last word?"

The Relational Origins of Embodied Action

Thus far we have focused on the way in meaning is continuously co-constructed in conversation. We must now expand the vision. After all, words are bodily actions, and except for analytic purposes, they should not be separated from physical activity. This is immediately evident when you consider sign language: the co-creation of meaning through gestures of the hands. Let us look at common conversation an embodied process of coordination – much like trapeze artists at work.

In the same way that our words are brought into meaning through co-action, so are the movements of our bodies. When newborn infants move their arms and legs in a seemingly aimless fashion, their movements are not meaning/full. That is, we don't see the movements as the infant's attempt to tell us something. By the time children reach the age of three, most all their movements will be culturally meaningful. Socialization is essentially a process of bringing the newborn into the patterns of commonly accepted coordination. When, where and how one speaks, smiles, weeps, shouts, walks, sits, runs, and the like are all given form and meaning within the process of relating. For example, when a friend is speaking to you, chances are that neither of you is standing on one leg, hopping about, or waving your arms. All these are possible actions, but all would be very strange. Chances are good, however, that you are both turned toward each other, and as one speaks the other may be nodding, smiling, grimacing, or otherwise matching facial expressions to the speaker's utterances. The actions of speaking and listening are like a dance: fully embodied coordination is essential.

Let's press this further: As you are talking with your friend, what are you wearing? If it's Saturday morning on the street, it might be jeans; if it's a swimming pool it might be a bathing suit, and if it's a wedding possibly a formal dress or tuxedo. It would not be easy to substitute garments across these occasions. It would be unusual, for example, to arrive at a wedding in a bathing suit. Because – just like the words we use – the way we dress acquires its meaning in a history of coordination. As Wittgenstein put it, our *language games* are embedded in our *forms of life*.[8] Now consider: If you removed everything from your life that did not have its origins in relational process, what would you do then? Precious little, I would imagine – perhaps breathing, digesting, sleeping, and other biological necessities. In short, we may trace *the source of all meaningful action to relational process*.

Co-Action and World Construction

As proposed, "making sense" is a collaborative activity – both in our words and actions. Now consider that in daily conversation we variously talk about ourselves, our family, friends, politics, sports, and so on. These are simply taken for granted realities. All the words

---

8. Ibid.

we use in these conversations are the outcomes of coordinated action. At the same time, we have generated agreements on when, how and where they are used. In the market' for example, we have agreed to name certain objects apples, and others grapes. Of course, these names are very useful in our everyday life, but we could have used other terms than "apples" and "grapes." Indeed, these words don't appear in languages other than English. In this sense the names are arbitrary; if it were useful we could call them "alphas" and "betas." Similarly, in the West, if we were to describe a man with his head in his hands and weeping, we might use such words as "sad" or "depressed." We would not generally describe him as "angry" or hungry," because that's not our tradition of naming on such occasions. This seems clear enough, but the implications are profound.

Most everyone would agree that apples and grapes are real, along with trees and mountains, deserts, the ocean, and so on. They all exist in the world, and they are not mythical or make-believe. But this is to engage in the *fallacy of misplaced concreteness*, treating words as if they were concrete objects or events. In effect, apples and grapes, trees, and mountains do not exist. Something may exist, but the words are simply useful in carrying out cultural life. Do alphas and betas exist? It seems strange to ask, but if we relied on these terms in referring to what we call apples and grapes, we would likely say that alphas and betas are undoubtedly real. The same applies to scientific knowledge. Such terms as atomic particles, chemical elements, osmosis, and economic growth were created within various communities to coordinate their activities. We make a mistake, however, to say that "atomic particles exist in the world." Scientific descriptions and explanations just happen to be useful for various communities in carrying out their work. And most important for our present concerns, without the process of co-action, we would not speak of individual persons at all. We speak of individuals as coming together to form a relationship, but it is within the process of coordination that the very idea of separate individuals was born. The idea of the independent individual has been useful for many purposes, but is perilous for charting our future.

These same proposals apply to what we call "good reasons" – or rationality. "Good reasons" are ways of talking that are valued by a group of people at a given time. What stands as a "rational choice" by one political party may be described as "dangerously misleading" by another. What stands as "good thinking" in one university class may be criticized as "too narrow and abstract" in another. Mathematical logics are generated within communities of agreement on what stands as logical within these communities. When we talk about ethics, morals, or values we are also participating in traditions of relationship. What we take to be moral in one tradition is immoral in another. Whether one travels miles to rally for justice, or to blow oneself up with a suicide bomb, depends one's history of relating. In short, *the source of all we take to be real, rational, and good is found in the process of relating*. Everything we believe or think, everything that is worth living or dying for is born, lives, or perishes in the process of coordination. If we are to survive together, attention to relational process is imperative.

Further Resources

Abib, M.A & Hesse, M.B. (1986) *The construction of reality*. Cambridge: Cambridge University Press.

Bellah, R.N., Madsen, R., Sullivan, W.M., Swidler, A. & Tipton, S.M. (1985) *Habits of the heart.* Berkeley, CA: University of California Press.

Garfinkel, H (1967) *Studies in Ethnomethodology*. Englewood Cliffs, NJ: Prentice Hall

Gergen, K.J. (2011) *Relational being: Beyond the individual and community*. New York: Oxford University Press.

Gergen, K.J. (2015) *An invitation to social construction*. London: Sage. 3rd. ed.

Latour, B. and Woolgar, S. (1979) *Laboratory life: The social construction of scientific facts*. London: Sage.

Leary, M.R. (2004) *The curse of the self: Self-awareness, egotism, and the quality of human life*. New York: Oxford University Press.

Linell, P. (2009) *Rethinking language, mind and world dialogically*. Charlotte, NC: Information Age.

Rosemont, H. 2015) *Against individualism*. A Confucian rethinking of the foundations of morality, politics, family and religion. Lanham, MD: Lexington Books.

Sampson, E.E (2008) *Celebrating the other: A dialogic account of human nature*. Chagrin Falls, OH: Taos Institute Publications.

Shapin, S. (1995). *A social history of truth: Civility and science in seventeenth-century England*. Chicago: University of Chicago Press.

Shotter, J. (1993) *Conversational realities: Constructing life through language*. London: Sage.

2. Living in the Relational Flow

Everything flows.

– Heraclitus

AS PROPOSED, THE LONGSTANDING ASSUMPTION that the social world is composed of independent entities lends itself to alienation, self-centeredness, hostility, and exploitation. Offered here is an alternative vision that traces the origins of all meaningful actions to a process in which we continuously participate. It is within this process that we become who we are. In this sense, *process precedes persons.* While the remaining chapters of this book explore the practical potentials of this vision, this chapter is devoted to expanding the conceptual resources. This is to deepen the understanding of relational process, thus providing tools for the further fashioning of practices. In the present chapter, we continue the focus on daily life. First introduced is the concept of multi-being, a way of understanding the person as a bearer of relational potentials. We then turn to the realization of these potentials in the process of relating. Of special concern are patterns that sustain, animate, and undermine our ways of living. We finally turn to the question of ethical value. From a relational perspective we open a new way of moving beyond ethical relativism.

Resources for Relating: Self as Multi-Being

I contain multitudes.

– Walt Whitman

Normally we think of individuals as coming together to form relationships. The individual exists; relationships are contrived. Here we are turning this truism on its head: It is out of relational process that what we call the person takes form. Whether we consider the essence of the person as a soul, a conscious decision-maker, or a brain in action depends on the tradition of meaning making in which we participate. Indeed, in the discourse of atomic physics, the material world does not contain persons. For present purposes, then, let us view human bodies as carrying *potentials for relational action.* Bodies both enable and limit our movements, but all they do in terms of meaningful action emerges from relational process. Let us explore.

Co-creating Potentials

As an adult, one may be able to read, write, tell stories, play games, be a loving mother or father, and so on. All are actions within the flow of relational process. As an infant, one had none of these potentials. There are many ways to explain how one moves from a relative state of incapacity to being skilled in these many ways. Here it is most useful to look at learning as a relational process. To sharpen the focus, let's say you are three years old and your mother is trying to teach you vocabulary. She takes out a book and opens it to a page with a picture of a bright red apple. She points to the image and says, "apple." As the two of you subsequently engage in a spiral of mutual coordination – attending, adjusting, mimicking, and so on – you acquire the capacity to speak the word "apple" in the presence of the image.

Simple enough. But consider that in this co-active process you have expanded your potentials in four ways: First, you have acquired a useful skill for participating in a commonly accepted use of the language. At the same time, however, while your mother is engaged in a full and complex array of actions – talking, smiling, pointing, and so on – you acquire the capacity to act as she does. Essentially, you exercise the capacity for imitation or *mimesis*. Even as adults, many of us can imitate what our mothers were like when we were children. Third, during this co-active process you emerge with the capacity to be a certain kind of person, a docile learner in this case who can say "apple" at an appropriate time. Finally, you emerge from the process with the capacity to engage in a process of relating, much like acquiring a way of dancing with a partner. In short, through the relational process, you can now *1) engage in a relationally useful action, 2) perform as the other, 3) perform as a particular self, and 4) engage in a form of self/other coordination.*

Now let's enlarge the sphere of relating. Let's add your relationship with a father, for example. Through this ongoing spiral of relating, you ultimately acquire useful skills, along with the potentials to perform like your father – to say the kinds of things he would say, respond to situations in the way he would respond. You also carry with you the kind of person(s) you became when you were with him – possibly respectful, fearful, rebellious, and so on. And you know how the process of coordination goes – who says what to whom in what order. You may also have brothers and sisters, each expanding your potentials for relational participation. And then there are the many friends and acquaintances over the years. Your way of laughing may resemble one, telling stories another, your clothing styles still others, along with perhaps your food preferences and tastes in music. Beyond these figures, there may be romantic partners, teachers, bosses, spiritual guides, and more. As the relational process spirals on, we may ever expand our potentials for coordinated action.

Such resources may also be acquired through our relations with the media – books, television, film, and so on. Consider here the way we read stories or watch movies. Typically, we imagine ourselves into one of the central roles in the story. For a brief period, we become the hero, the sleuth, the lover, and so on. We may share their aspirations, their fears, their bravery, and their heartbreaks. Most importantly, we acquire the potential to act as we imagine they would, to be brave, loving bold, crafty and so on. We may carry with us the potentials to be both saints and sinners, police and thieves, or gender fluid.

In sum, we emerge from a history of relating as *multi-beings*. We carry with us enormous potentials for action, even if only a fraction may ever be played out on the stage of life. As we move through a day, many of these resources are drawn into action – in relating with a friend, a colleague, a parent, a child, a customer, a lover, and so on.

Accumulated Potentials for Action

Vistas of Becoming

As we move through the day, we are ever immersed in relational process. Even when others are not physically present, our activities are carried out within the understandings acquired within that process. Whatever "makes sense'" finds its origins in co-creation. Let us focus here, however, on face-to-face encounters and the merging of multi-beings. Each may contain multitudes, but in the moment of meeting the challenge of coordinating action is set in motion. The participants each draw from their acquired resources, and whatever is said or done by either party is given meaning through the other's words and actions. In each moment, their potentials are brought into play and counter-play. As the process proceeds, subtle and unspoken agreements emerge on what is reasonable and valuable; the participants each acquire a particular identity. A small but fleeting universe is under construction.

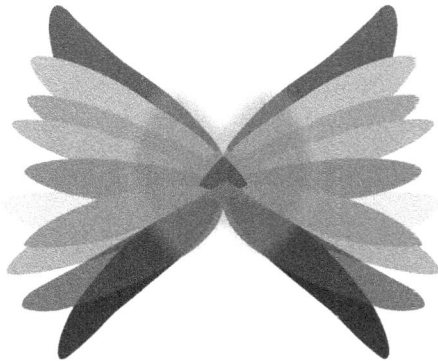

One might imagine each multi-being as carrying a wing of potentials, much like a butterfly. But it is only together that they can take flight. At the same time, they do not fly freely. There are first the limits of their potentials. It is difficult to have a conversation, for example, if there is no shared language, and one can scarcely raise a voice of critique if one only knows how to be obedient. Also limiting are what one might call habits. These are potentials so frequently used that the alternatives are brushed aside or seem alien. Most people learn, for example, how to perform one of two genders, and would revolt if required to switch genders – even if they know very well how to "be the other." In this context, we can also understand why many feel there is a true or core self. With the habitual exercise of a potential, it comes to be "who I really am."

Yet, we should not let this focus on limits cloud over the richness of the resources, the continuous learning, or the situational variations. As we move across the plain of daily life, we also move across relationships. We encounter friends, children, intimate partners, colleagues, children, and so on, and in each case different potentials are brought into the relational dance. As the famous psychologist William James once wrote, "There are as many social selves as there are distinct groups or persons about whose opinion one cares."[9] While there is much to say on these matters, let's focus on two particular issues that follow from these views.

Understanding as Relational Coordination

For centuries Western scholars have struggled with the question of how we understand others' minds. How do we know what others are thinking or feeling; how can we ascertain their motives and intentions? Of course, in daily life we more or less assume that people can tell us about their thoughts and feelings, and their behavior will

---

9. James, W.(1890) *Principles of psychology*. New York: Henry Holt.

reveal their motives. But now the pesky question emerges: how can we actually know what these words and actions are expressions *of*? When people declare their love for each other, for example, how do they know they are feeling the same way? They have no access to each other's internal worlds; perhaps they mean totally different things – mild attraction, physical passion, spiritual connection, or….? And if one tried to clarify, "oh, it means I adore you," what do those words reflect inside his head? A buzzing excitement, physical passion…? For centuries scholars have sought an answer to this puzzle, but there is no satisfactory solution as to how one can identify what's going on inside another's mind from external expressions. Indeed, how can we be certain that there *are* minds inside people's heads? Or in the words of feminist scholar Judith Butler, why should we suppose there is a "doer behind the deed"?[10]

From the present perspective, the traditional problem of under-standing is ill-framed. It is premised on the assumption of separa-tion: independent individuals whose activities issue from somewhere behind the eyeballs. In contrast, we begin here with the relational process and people's potentials for coordination. As the social theo-rist John Shotter would say, "Instead of asking what's inside one's head, let us ask what relationships one's head is inside of."[11] Here we can answer the question of understanding in terms of successful coordination.

Consider some cases in which someone seems to misunderstand: you see a man smoking in a prohibited area, you ask a dinner com-

10. Butler, J. (1990) *Gender trouble. Feminism and the subversion of identity*. London: Routledge.
11. Shotter, J. (2008) *Conversational Realities Revisited*. Chagrin Falls, OH: Taos Insti-tute Publications.

panion to "please pass the salt," and she passes a plate of salmon, you pay a complement to a friend and he accuses you of manipulation. In none of these cases can you see into the mind of the other. All you have is the public action. The conclusion that these are misunderstandings rests on the fact that the actions do not fit within an anticipated or acceptable pattern of coordination. *When people understand each other, they are not reading minds but participating in congenial patterns of relating.* If you feel a complex book of philosophy defies your understanding, it is not because you cannot grasp what's in the head of the philosopher. It is not being sure of an appropriate way of responding. It's similar to being asked to join a dance you have never heard of. Understanding people from other cultures is akin to finding a mutually agreeable way to dance together.

Comfort and Containment: Dramas of Everyday Life

This view of understanding as congenial coordination raises a second important issue. Why are misunderstandings, disappointments, frustrations, and the related dramas of everyday life so prevalent? After all, we find a strong tendency among people to find a mutually comfortable pattern of relating. People meet and soon search for topics about which they can congenially talk. Their movements and facial expressions signal mutual understanding. Out of such coordination may emerge friendships, partnerships, marriages, and so on. Over time, the participants begin to count on these reliable ways of relating. In close relationships, a couple may sustain patterns of eating, sleeping, and conversing together for decades. Here we also find the origin of trust, safety, and tranquility – a sense of truly knowing each other. For many, these are treasures.

But herein lies the irony: as we coordinate toward comfort, we simultaneously set in motion the potentials for its disruption. As we move across the day – in friendship and family circles, on the job, in places of worship, at the club – these same tendencies toward harmonious coordination will also be in motion. In each context, participants will coordinate their actions as needed. They will acquire particular identities – as mother, father, teacher, student, friend, lover, colleague, boss, political activist, artist, and so on. And in each context, a small universe will be under construction, with its particular realities, rationalities, and values. Further, within these encounters, the participants may have little access to the full range of universes in which each other is engaged. The dominating reality is here and now, and the full range of other selves, their significance, their strangeness, or acceptability, may be obscured.

Placed in these terms, it is easy to see how many of the disruptive dramas of daily life emerge. Achieving harmony at work may interfere with the accord of homelife, which may disrupt trusted bonds of friendship, which cast doubt on one's commitment to a team, a club, or political group. Issues of trust, loyalty, jealousy, identity, and security all lurk within the shadows of our daily relationships. Even the turn of a phrase may be sufficient to bring them to life. In brief, *the well-being of any relationship ultimately rests on its coordination with other relationships.* It is challenging enough to achieve harmony in any given relationship; we are far less prepared for the dances essential to harmonious living in the multiple and ever-expanding worlds of relating.

Making Worlds Together

As we see, the common quest for coordinated action does not necessarily lead to harmony. We co-create good and meaningful lives in the same way we co-create exploitation, injustice, and aggression. A friendship, a partnership, and a loving family relationship are all relational achievements, but so are robberies and murders. We are not lone agents in the world, choosing our paths as we see them; together we make our paths as we proceed. Let us focus then on some of the micro-processes by which we make these worlds together. In doing so, we open possibilities for creating new and more promising paths.

Relational Patterning: Scenarios

While continuously making worlds together, we are mainly drawing from the resources supplied by past relationships. Thus, as I write these lines, I am drawing from traditions long past. Words, grammar, and paragraph structures… all are variations on what my relational history has supplied me. If this were not so, you as reader would have difficulty in understanding me. The sources of our making sense together were generated long before our births; they are now so commonplace as to be unnoticeable. This also means that we carry with us an enormous reservoir of know-how in terms of moment-to-moment relating. Consider a friend who thanks you for your help. You are not suddenly dumb-struck, wondering what to say now. Rather, you may unhesitatingly reply, "Oh, you're welcome," or "It was nothing really." More broadly, then, we participate in common traditions of relating. Let us define such patterns as *relational scenarios*.

Many scenarios are very brief. For example,

A: Asks a question

B: Answers the question

A: Makes a proposal

B: Argues against the proposal

A: Asks for help

B: Provides help

A: Tells a joke

B: Laughs

You can also appreciate the power of such simple scenarios by imagining what life would be like should they be violated. In any of these cases, what if Person B responded by sobbing loudly, hopping on one foot, or reporting on the weather in Lapland. Daily life proceeds as smoothly as it does primarily because we repeat the familiar scenarios.[12]

Other scenarios are much longer in duration. For example, courtship in many societies is highly patterned and may take months to complete. Like theater, the couple's family members understand the parts they play and when specific actions are appropriate. Cycles of revenge can be played out over centuries, for example when a family or a group takes revenge for what they see as injustice, only to find that the target now feels justified in retaliating, thus re-establishing a reason for revenge.

We move daily through an extended flow of relational action,

12. Garfinkel, H. (1967) *Studies in ethnomethodology*. Englewood Cliffs, NJ, Prentice-Hall

and through the process of coordination our lives take shape. Here it is useful to focus on four general patterns of coordination and their significance to our becoming:

Sustaining Scenarios

While unremarkable, most of our ordinary, everyday interchanges enable us to go on in satisfactory and predictable ways. Simple greetings – such as "Hi, how are you doing today?" followed by "Fine, what about you?" – are sustaining scenarios, as are exchanges of "good-bye" at the end of the day, paying attention while another is speaking, and other simple exchanges of politeness. What we call "small talk" is similar. Such conversations have little instrumental value; the light and pleasant banter is sufficient in itself. But the importance of such conversations shouldn't be underestimated. The interchange may seem superficial, simply the background for the "important issues." But in many ways, these simple rituals are the glue holding daily life together.

Generative Scenarios

Given the groundwork of sustaining scenarios, consider those conversations that seem to "go somewhere." There is a spark, excitement, delight, or possibly a sense of growth, renewal, or inspiration. Generative scenarios are those in which the trajectory moves in a positive direction for the participants. Such interchanges may be brief, intermittent, or extended, but it is here that we ascend from the ordinary toward the extraordinary. How is it that these meaningful, joyful, or enriching episodes are brought into being? Some might say, "it's the chemistry," or it's merely luck. And to be sure, there is no simple answer to this question. History, culture, and local conditions can all play a role. However, from a relational standpoint one gains insight by looking at the actions making up the scenario. For example, if asked about some of the actions that characterize interchanges of this kind, you might include acts of agreement, support, gratitude, sharing, and affection. However, these are not stand-alone actions; for example, out of any conversational context the excited expression "Oh, thank you so much" is nonsensical. Attention thus moves to the patterns of coordination in which such actions would make sense. Consider, for example:

A: Expresses an opinion

B: Agrees with the opinion

A: Reveals a weakness

B: Expresses sympathy

A: Gives a gift

B: Expresses gratitude

A: Expresses interest in an activity

B: Shares enthusiasm for the activity

A: Expresses affection for B

B: Expresses affection for A

In these brief scenarios, we find the potential for positive or generative movement in the relationship. One might even build a vocabulary of coordinated actions for positive growth in relating – in personal relations, in classrooms, offices, hospitals, or in relations between police and citizens. To be sure, there are significant differences among people in their histories of relating, and the potentials they bring to a given situation. In this sense, generative coordination is fundamentally an art. But if the flow is in the positive direction, there are two factors that lend support to the trajectory:

Self-Reinforcement. One of the intriguing insights developed by communication theorists is the way in which scenarios can be self-reinforcing. That is, a positive exchange of actions invites the continuation of that same pattern. Suppose A's expression of affection, for example, is followed by B's reciprocal expression of appreciation. In that case, A may be encouraged to express affection on later occasions, with the likely response that B will reciprocate. The pattern thus repeats itself. As many family therapists see it, such circular scenarios are key to healthy family relationships. Within a group or organization, such circularity also contributes to high morale and solidarity.

Diffusion. The circular tendency of many relational scenarios is significant in building and sustaining friendships, family bonds, and thriving organizational cultures. Yet, we must also recognize the ways in which generative scenarios build upon each other. One positive exchange opens the way to others. In the above cases, for example, if B expresses appreciation for A's opinion, A may become more trusting of B. This sense of trust might open the way to A's revealing a weakness. And if B is then sympathetic, A may send a small gift to B. In effect, positive scenarios lend themselves to further positive scenarios so there is a diffusion of generativity. Here we set the stage for a major shift from the ordinary to the extraordinary – to periods of enthusiasm, delight, and discovery.

Degenerative Scenarios

In familiar contrast to such upward swings in relating are patterns of deterioration. Shadowing the landscape of cultural life are heated arguments, anger, jealousy, blame, bullying, prejudice, and exploitation, – at home, school, and the workplace. More globally, we co-create war, terrorism, and endless cycles of aggression and retaliation. Degenerative scenarios are relational sequences that move their participants from silent animosity to mutual annihilation. Movement in this direction may be triggered by the next turn in a conversation. To illustrate, return to the generative sequences just discussed, and consider the way in which B's response opens the way to relational deterioration:

A: Expresses an opinion

B: Attacks the opinion

A: Reveals a weakness

B: Ridicules the weakness

A: Gives a gift

B: Criticizes the gift

A: Expresses interest in an activity

B: Scorns the activity

A: Expresses affection for B

B: Expresses indifference

Here it is useful to consider each turn in a conversation as a *pivot point*. That is, the moment we begin to take our turn in the conversation we stand at a point in which our next utterance may shift the direction of relating in a positive or negative direction. And too, we may also find deadening repetitions if the direction is negative. Attacking each other's opinions, for example, has become a cultural pastime. We may also find a diffuse spreading of degenerative scenarios throughout a relationship. Bitter arguments may invite subsequent expressions of ridicule, scorn, and indifference.

Family therapist Karl Tomm calls attention to the circular character of many degenerative scenarios.[13] As he sees it, these continuing practices of relating are forms of family pathology. Consider, for example, several pathologizing scenarios that frequently occur in relationships between a parent and an adolescent son or daughter:

Parent		Adolescent
Criticizing	⟷	Defending
Judging	⟷	Protesting
Questioning	⟷	Avoiding Answering

To underscore the self-reinforcing circularity, when a parent criticizes her daughter, the adolescent may well defend what she is doing, which then invites her mother to intensify the critique, which again invites the adolescent's mounting defense. Many of these circular scenarios are so common that we "just naturally" participate. Communication specialists point out that we may continue such painful patterns even when we know it.[14] We repeat them, not only because they are familiar, but because we don't know what else to do.

---

13. Tomm, K. (2014) *Patterns in interpersonal interactions: Inviting relational understandings for therapeutic change.* New York: Routledge.
14. Cronen, V.E., Pearce, W.B., and Snavely, L.M. (1980) A theory of role-structure and types of episodes and study of perceived enmeshment in undesired repetitive patterns ("URPSs") *Communication Yearbook,* 3, 225-240.

Regenerative Scenarios

The route to degeneration is always at hand. So long as we place a value on anything, there will be the devalued, the less than good, the unwanted. And as the criteria of the good expand, so will the invitations to scold, criticize, or attack. At the same time, however, because degenerative scenarios are so prevalent, humans have also created scenarios for returning to normal, "patching things up," making peace, and the like. These regenerative scenarios are crucially important in the present era. With the world's peoples now confronting each other as never before, the potentials for alienation and animosity are pervasive. It is easy enough for people to avoid, distrust, or disparage those who are "different." Degeneration is effortless; restoration is an increasing challenge.

To explore the dynamics of restoration, consider a common slide into animosity, the scenario of mutual blame. Person A accuses B of irresponsibility, a failing, the cause of defeat, or some unfortunate event. In reply, B turns and blames A for the outcome. "It wasn't my fault this happened; it was yours..." Most frequently, A then denies the accusation and elaborates further on B's failings. Now B responds by further denial and elaboration of A's obvious irresponsibility. The exchange of mutual blame continues until...? And this is indeed the question: how do participants who are moving toward mutual animosity restore their relationship?

Here we focus again on the pivot points. At any juncture in the scenario, the next utterance may disrupt the downward spiral, and shift the trajectory. In effect, one may respond to an accusation of blame in a way that invites restoration in the relationship. Of course, once caught up in the familiar "blame game," such possibilities may seem remote. In the heat of battle, who thinks to kiss the enemy? However, in the arts of relating, a hovering consciousness of possibilities is a precious resource. Consider then some potentially promising options for responding to another's accusations:

- Apologizing
- Admitting partial responsibility
- Explaining how blame is not warranted for either party
- Making a joke of the way they are blaming each other
- Silence

Perhaps you the reader, can still add further possibilities. With a little brainstorming, new paths toward restoration could be created. For example, a family therapist might ask, "Isn't there a better way for us to talk about this?" The important point is that mutual blame is not a fixed scenario; rather than playing by the rules, we must play *with* the rules.[15]

Scaffolds of Suffering and Support

At the same time that we are free to shift the direction of a given scenario and to co-construct new ways of going on, there are conditions that invite or encourage one form as opposed to another. They don't determine our ways of relating, but they provide scaffolds of support. To take an obvious case, in courts of law we have erected a scaffold inviting contentious argument. That is, we have established a courtroom tradition which prosecutors and defense lawyers are set against

---

15. Carse, J. P. (1987) *Finite and infinite games: A vision of life as play and possibility.* New York: Ballentine.

each other. In the process of relating, they are invited into continuous and unabated disagreement. Similarly, to help voters in deciding on candidates, debates between candidates are often arranged. In the process of debate it is "just normal" for the contenders to justify or glorify themselves and criticize the "opponent." But here we must realize that in both these cases we have scaffolded a degenerative process of relating. Regardless of the private doubts of the lawyers, or the vast areas of agreement among the politicians, we have scaffolded a relational process in which they will become antagonists. And here we must ask, is justice truly served in. our courts of law by unswerving contention. And in the political arena, is the greater good of a country served by scaffolding antagonism?

Such questions set the stage for a major concern of this book. What kinds of relational processes are scaffolded by our institutions? How do our schools, businesses, hospitals, religious institutions, police forces, and governments invite or constrain our forms of relating? What kinds of relations do we set in motion when we scaffold competition for wealth; when some people are granted power over others; or national policies are determined by competing political parties? How are we served? What promise do our forms of relating hold for the future? What alternatives can we create together?

Toward a Relational Ethic

Such questions can scarcely be answered from a value-neutral standpoint. In asking about our wishes for the future, we are asking about what we care about; what is a good way of life? It is easy enough to answer such questions in the abstract. Of course, don't we all want peace, happiness, prosperity, and the like? But in the daily practices of living the question is far from simple. In all corners of the world we are engaged in co-creating satisfactory forms of life. The resulting variations are enormous, and thus result in the continuing and often bitter conflicts. Recognizing these differences, humans have long attempted to create ethical standards, or moral codes for living. If we only had a code of ethics, it is proposed, we could make sound judgments in comparing ways of life. We could say that it is better for people to live this way as opposed to that.

Yet, in spite of our centuries of searching for ethical certainty – whether in the form of a philosophy, religious creed, or political doctrine – the question remains open, disagreement continues, and conflict abounds. Worse still, such certainties about "the good" have often functioned to suppress – or eradicate – those who disagree. How then should we proceed?

As many propose, we should respect these variations. People create multiple ways of life, and these ways of life hold value for them – each within their own history, culture and context. "We should honor these many traditions," it is argued, and "avoid proclaiming any one way of life as ethically or morally superior to another." While this sounds reasonable, those seeking certainty are repulsed. "Are you saying that one tradition is just as good as another?" they ask. "If we accept that kind of relativism, we would have to accept slavery, genocide, the Holocaust, and dropping atom bombs on innocent people. After all, aren't these just people's ways of expressing their values?" As we see, neither absolutist ethics nor ethical relativism offer a satisfactory way forward.

Let us consider a third possibility. In the preceding chapter we traced the origins of our traditions to relational process, and this included their cherished values and moralities. So, while the variations in traditions of value are enormous, the one thing they share is the relational process by which they were given birth. By the same token, should the relational process be terminated, so would their valued way of life. It is here that we can locate the possibility of a universal ethic that accommodates the infinite variations. Regardless of the forms of life to which we are variously allied, it is the wellbeing of the relational process that holds ethical primacy. Thus, when traditions of the good come into conflict, the point is not to enter into an argument over which is the better, or whether one is evil while to other is good. The argumentative process will itself drive the contenders apart. Rather, the answer lies in locating or creating a relational process that will enable us to go on together. The universal ethic is not then a remote abstraction, but lived out in our practices of relating.

In the remaining chapters we must ask whether the relational processes embedded in our major institutions are sufficient for their continued survival. Do these processes contribute to the wellbeing of the participants, or to global wellbeing more generally? Hovering above all, however, is the question of whether the process of relating is itself enriched.

Further Resources

Bavelas, J. , Gerwing, J. & Healing., S. (2017) Doing mutual understanding. Calibrating with micro-sequences in face-to-face dialogue. *Journal of Pragmatics.* 121: 91-112.

Gergen, K.J. (2019) Toward a relational ethic. In H. Alma & I. Avest (Eds.) *Moral and spiritual leadership in an age of plural moralities.* London:Routledge.

Hermans, H.J.M. (2018). *Society in the self: A theory of identity in democracy.* New York: Oxford University Press.

Romaioli, D. (2013*). La terapia multi-being. Una prospettiva relazionale in psicoterapia.* Chagrin Falls, OH: Taos Institute Worldshare Books.

Schegloff, E.A. (2007) *Sequence organization in interaction: A primer in conversation analysis.* Cambridge: Cambridge University Press.

Shotter, J. (2008) *Conversational Realities Revisited.* Chagrin Falls, OH: Taos Institute Publications.

Stewart, J. (2013) *U&ME: Communicating in moments that matter.* Chagrin Falls, OH: Taos Institute.

Tomm, K., St. George, S., Wulff, D., & Strong, T. (2014) *Patterns in interpersonal interactions: Inviting relational understandings for therapeutic change.* New York: Routledge.

Wasserman, I.C. & Fisher-Yoshida, B. (2017). *Communicating possibilities: A brief introduction to the coordinated management of meaning (CMM).* Chagrin Falls, OH: Taos Institute.

3. Education as Relational Process

*No significant learning occurs
without significant relationship.*

– James P. Comer

IN A WORLD OF INCREASINGLY rapid change, opportunity, and disruption, how are we to deal with the complexity, the conflict, and the challenges of living in a world of multiple values and visions? What prevents us from moving further toward a world in which individuals, organizations, and nations are out for *me first?* These are crucial questions for the future of education. Our schools may be the single most important source of preparation for moving forward together. Are they up to the challenge? Consider:

> You are a 14 year old sitting at your desk in a classroom The teacher is handing out the final exam for the mathematics course. Her chair is placed at the head of the class to prevent cheating. You know you aren't really prepared, partly because you didn't have time to study and partly because the subject and the teacher are boring. But you need to make a good score. If you fail, your parents will punish you, and your friends will think you are stupid. And to make matters worse, two more exams are coming this week. It feels like prison.

This is a grim picture, but for all too many it is normal school life. The day is mostly regimented, the subject matter has little interest, and your job is to absorb information for which you will be judged by the teacher, your parents, and your classmates. You are weary, frustrated, and anxious about your performance.

How did this way of life come to be? In Western culture this approach to education can be traced to the Industrial Revolution of the early 1900s, and is often linked to the image of schools as factories. Like factories, schools take in raw materials and shape them into a desired product. The products are then consumed by various employers. Like a good factory, the teachers work on the assembly line, with the principal as "the boss." Tests and exams are used for quality control, and the success of the factory is assessed through a cost/benefit analysis. "How can schools function at top efficiency, with high production and low costs"?

Discontent with this form of schooling is massive. It is not only the students' boredom, stress, and alienation, along with the skyrocketing numbers treated for mental disorders or who drop from the system altogether. There is also the question of whether they are learning anything relevant to the complex, rapidly changing and unpredictable circumstances now confronting us. Where, it is asked, are they developing their creative potentials, a love of learning, and the ability to relate well with others in a multi-cultural world? Yet, while there is little love for the factory orientation to education, the model remains dominant. It has yet to be challenged by a compelling alternative.

In this chapter we thus explore a vision of education as a process of relating. This process is at the center of education. We become enthusiastic about a topic largely through our relationships; whether we learn or not depends importantly on our relationship with the teacher, classmates, and family; what counts as good reasoning or intelligent action depends on who is judging. And if one fails an exam, why do we blame the student? Why not the teacher, the curriculum, one's parents, or the fear of failure that the exam situation evokes? One does not succeed or fail alone. There is also the broader network of relations in which schooling takes place – most immediately with family, friends and community, but as well with the larger society, and onward to the global community. And too, what takes place within these relationships cannot be disconnected from the environment – school buildings, rooms, facilities, the quality of air, available food and so on.

In what follows we focus mainly on human relationships, and consider the possibility of replacing the industrial model of education with a relation centered orientation. What would education look like; what outcomes might result? There is much to say on this topic, with relevant dialogues now spanning the globe. Inspiring practices now point the way to the future.

The Relational Goal of Education

The purpose of public education has been long debated, but many would agree with John Dewey's general vision: education should prepare the new generations for participation in society.[16] From a relational standpoint, we may see this as *enabling participation in the positive flow of coordinated action*. This is to place the focus of education neither on developing the individual, nor enhancing the

---

16. Dewey, J. (1897) "My pedagogic creed," *School Journal*, 54: 77–80.

society, but on relational processes for sustaining and creating flourishing forms of life. While neglecting neither the individual nor the learning of specific subject matters, it is to see these in the context of the vital challenges increasingly confronting the world. Needed are capacities for moving effectively in conditions of rapid and ambiguous change, for innovation, conjoining traditions, repairing conflict, and co-creating new forms of life.

In these terms, our traditional orientation to education is deeply troubling. The forms of relating scaffolded by the vision of schools as factories, undermines these very aims. The process is lodged in the assumption of persons as bounded or separated units, each assigned and evaluated in terms of performing a particular function. Most obviously, each student is assessed on scholastic performance. However, teachers are also held individually responsible for their efficacy, as are school administrators, schools, and entire national systems of education. At each level there is also competition, thus thrusting students, teachers, and schools into antagonism. At the student level, this also creates a tension between high and low performers, with each seeing the other as defective (as simple-minded on the one side and arrogant on the other). Traditional education does less to enrich relational potentials than it does to destroy them.

Relationally Enriched Learning

Given these aims of education how should we proceed? What would this mean for the learning process? What kinds of pedagogical or teaching practices would be invited? What would happen to curricula, textbooks, lesson plans and the like? Are there new roles for the teacher, and new ways of thinking about students, their families, and communities? These are not invitations to fantasy. Indeed, the concerns raised here are shared by creative educators around the world. Innovations are everywhere in motion, and many of them are consistent with the relational view outlined here.

To glimpse the possibilities, let us build on the work of a highly successful school system in Norway. From their practices we can draw out several significant themes with implications for relationally enriched learning. The Youth Invest schools in Norway confront one of the most difficult challenges in education today: student dropouts. For teeming numbers of adolescents across many countries, school has become intolerable. They cease to attend. Yet, by dropping out they also jeopardize their future, along with the well-being of the nation itself. In terms of restoring the educational interests of dropouts, the Youth Invest system has been an outstanding success.[17] Not only do the dropouts return to the school, they enthusiastically participate in the educational process. The program has become a model for schools across the country. As the school attracts international attention, many educators see the implications of the Youth Invest program for education more generally. Why just dropouts? In terms of relational process, the program's success may be understood in terms of three major features.

From Products to Partnerships

The factory metaphor of education implies that students are essentially raw material to be shaped by the educational system. The relationship of the teaching staff to students is thus defined in

17. Maeland, I. (2020) Creating new futures through collaboration: Dropouts no more. In McNamee et al (Eds) *The Sage handbook of social constructionist practice*. London: Sage Publications.

causal terms: *we* shape *you*. The relationship is fundamentally alienating, with intimidation serving as the primary means of motivating students: *perform or fail!* To ensure the quality of "the product," teachers and parents become instruments of surveillance and control. In contrast, consider some of the practices cultivated by the Youth Invest program. Abandoning the definition of students as objects to be shaped, the primary emphasis is on generating an ethos of partnership. Partnerships should not only include relationships between teachers and students, but among students, and with the school community as a whole. Consider some relevant practices:

- The common distinction between students and teachers suggests a distance between two groups, along with a separation of roles. In the Youth Invest program students are called *young learning colleague*s. The stress is placed on how both students and teachers learn from each other.

- Building a partnership entails removing the judgmental orientation that has crippled many students, and providing them with a caring interest in their wellbeing. When students have problems they wish to discuss, the emphasis is placed on their capabilities and potentials instead of their shortcomings and limitations.

- When the students give reports or presentations in front of a class, their classmates are furnished with *strength cards*, each printed with a positive or admirable quality. After the presentation, classmates have the opportunity to give the presenter one or more of these cards. The presenter may learn, for example, that he or she has courage, offers hope, or is creative.

- School policy meetings are scheduled throughout the year, and these meetings systematically include students in the discussions.

- Students frequently attend conferences together with their
  teachers and staff, often joining them in public presentations.

Many other forward-looking schools are moving toward relations
of partnership. Indeed, many schools are now exploring *strength-
based approaches* to education. As many realize, the common focus
on students' failures – wrong answers, poor attention, irresponsible
behavior – is not only personally deflating, but distances them from
their teachers. In contrast, when attention is paid to their competen-
cies, interest in learning and relationships with teachers blossom.
Closely related are *appreciative* practices of social change, many of
which have been used for school transformation around the world.[18]
More will be said about appreciative inquiry in Chapter 5, but the
central fulcrum of change lies in generating conversation on what is
valued or appreciated as opposed to "what is wrong" in the situation.

In one interesting application, students focused on their appreciation for their mentors.[19] A mentor did not necessarily have to be a
teacher, but could be anyone who had made a positive difference in
their lives. As part of a class assignment, each wrote in detail about
the way this individual had affected them. Small details on their
kindness and character could be included. As it turned out, students
wrote about a wide range of individuals, including for example a
childhood baby-sitter, an athletic trainer, a second language teacher,
and a woman who worked in the school cafeteria. Later, a ceremony
was arranged at the school in which all those featured in the essays

18. Dole, D., Godwin, L. & Moehle, M. (Eds.) (2014) *Exceeding expectations: An
anthology of appreciative inquiry stories in education.* Chagrin Falls, OH: Taos Institute
Publications.
19. Wade, J. (2014) Kindness units us: Junior high students appreciating their mentors. In Dole et al. *ibid.*

were invited to listen to the students present their testimonials. The result was a feast of good will, and the "Kindness Unites Us" project became a beacon for other schools.

From Cookie-Cutter to Co-Creation

When schools are treated as factories, the educational machinery is designed to produce a standard product of high quality – perfect cookies, cut to specification. Consistent with this image, most public schools follow a standardized curriculum, and are subject to national testing and international comparisons. This embrace of standardization has long been questioned, but is now under sharp attack. In a context of rapid and complex global change, a cookie-cutter approach to education is dangerous. Needed are wide variations in skills, knowledge, and passions; standardization is the enemy. Nor does standardization recognize the global flow of meaning-making, with ideas, ideologies and innovations moving silently and unpredictably across geographic borders. Standardization is insensitive to the richly varied and continuously changing circumstances of the world.

More broadly, what is invited from a relational perspective is an educational process sensitive to students' needs, aspirations, skills, and values, along with the conditions, and opportunities of the time. The point is not to produce standard students, but to facilitate and encourage rich and varied trajectories of learning and development. In this light, consider a central practice of the Youth Invest schools: student *Road Maps*. In most public schools, teachers must administer a standard course curriculum, regardless of its relevance to their wisdom or the students' interests. Students are initially asked to consider, "where would you like to see yourself in five years?" A student might reply that he would like to be a mechanic for luxury cars and to have a companion, an apartment, and perhaps a dog. These dreams are then placed at the top of a large scroll of paper. The interview then continues to consider what steps would be needed to achieve this dream. What kinds of learning would be required; what courses might be needed? As the two of them converse, they add these steps on a large piece of paper.

To illustrate, the two might agree that it is essential to have a driver's license, auto repair classes, some ability to read and do math, and so on. As each of these needs becomes clear, the student also realizes the immediate steps he needs to take – courses, workshops, and so on. When the Youth Invest School cannot provide these offerings, the interviewer guides the way to resources available at neighboring schools or the community. Importantly, the interviewer also asks the student about who is needed to help or support him along the way. It may become clear, for example, that the student would benefit from the support of his teachers, other students, his parents, and possibly some members of the community.

This information may also be added to the map. In order to keep this path to the future alive and relevant, it is posted on the wall of the school for all to share. Where there was once a sullen and alienated young man, there is now an individual engaged in his studies, with a positive sense of his goals, what he needs to reach them, and an appreciation of others.

The Youth Invest Schools are not alone in their attempt to escape the *one size fits all curricula* that dominate public education. Such attempts have important beginnings in the child-centered orientation in kindergarten and primary schools. Owing especially to the innovative work in Montessori schools and the Reggio Emilia School in Italy, practices of *emergent curricula* have become visible. Rather than establishing a fixed curriculum plan for classes as a whole, attention turns to each child's curiosities and talents. Where one child is fascinated with undersea life, another might enjoy painting or designing dresses. In each case, teachers work with the children to help develop their interests. The term *collective curricula* is applied to practices in which children decide together what they might wish to explore as a group. A small class might thus meet in the morning to develop a plan for the day. Would it be interesting to plan a garden, for example, or to explore the origins of the milk they are drinking? Group discussion determines the direction.

Of course, while flexible curricula seem reasonable for young children, many question their relevance to adolescent education. Here, education becomes "serious business," as parents and policy makers consider the adequacy of education in preparing the young for future occupations. At the same time, however, it is broadly recognized that standardized education is poor preparation for working in a world in which flexibility, varied skills, and innovation are essential. Such concerns have stimulated the growth of *project based learning practices.* Here a real-world problem is typically identified, and the teacher acts as a facilitator to the students' attempts to solve it. For younger students the challenge might be to make a map that would guide them to a favorite destination, or to generate a recipe for a cake that they bake for the class; as students grow older the tasks become more complex, such as designing a recycling system for the school, or building a computer. Students are thus challenged with bringing together various forms of knowledge, then reflecting, synthesizing, experimenting, and evaluating.

Project based learning can be carried out alone or with others, and in both cases the outcomes are typically presented to others. Often, the results are conveyed orally, visually, or using multi-media. The audience may include classmates, teaching staff, parents and community members. At some schools, a fair is offered to the public at the end of the school year. Here students may converse with interested visitors to their project sites. Project based learning is rapidly gaining adherents around the world. A beacon for the movement is the HighTech High network of California schools where the curriculum from elementary to high school is almost exclusively built around project based learning. In these schools, one can scarcely locate a textbook, rows of desks in a classroom, or written tests.

From Monologue to Dialogue

Critics see traditional education as designed to stuff knowledge into the heads of ignorant students. Traditional teaching, then, often takes the form of a monologue in which teachers lecture students about what they must know. Students are thus trained to be passive receptacles – taking notes, memorizing, regurgitating – but otherwise treated as if they have nothing to offer. In striking contrast students in the Youth Invest program are invited to participate as partners in their education. They discuss their hopes and needs; they share their opinions with faculty and friends; and classes are buzzing with conversation. This introduces the third characteristic of relationally enriched learning: *the centrality of dialogue*. The importance of dialogic learning cannot be over-emphasized. Its advantages over monologue typically include the ways in which participants can:

- *acquire knowledge* not only relevant to the subject matter, but also about others' perspectives, opinions, and values. Understanding of others' lifeways and cultural conditions expands.

- *develop skills in co-creating*. Capacities are expanded for sharing ideas, raising questions, discussing differences, and so on. Acquired here are resources for participating in generative processes of relating.

- *realize the value of relational process itself*. Concerns with *me* and *mine* can be replaced with an appreciation of what *we* can generate together.

Of course, not all dialogues are so generous in their outcomes. Conversations can be superficial, incoherent, and contentious. In traditional dialogic teaching, often identified as Socratic, the teacher often controls or constrains the proceedings, thus moving the class toward a preferred conclusion. The result is often discrimination between those who make preferred as opposed to "irrelevant" contributions. Such dialogue can also be dominated by a few articulate or ambitious students, with the timid discouraged from speaking at all. Many educators thus experiment with modifications, with particular sensitivity to issues of inclusion, power dynamics, and equalized participation. This shift is represented in the global development of *collaborative (or cooperative) learning* practices, in which two or more students learn together. For example, young children may create a collective painting, draw a map together of the neighborhood, or share stories about a particular event or topic. Older students might create a video together or lead the class in an exploration. At the university level, groups may be invited to interpret a text or solve a complex problem together, and then share their opinions with the class. The creative possibilities are endless.

In shifting from a factory to a relational orientation to education, an emphasis has so far been placed on partnering with students, co-creating curricula, and dialogic learning. Yet, the flourishing of these movements is obstructed in one major way: the demands for standardized assessment. If education is an ever-moving process of relating, why should a summary judgment be placed on an *individual's* performance? Why should we rank individuals or place grades on their worth, and in a pluralist world who can claim the authority to do so? Let us explore the implications.

Beyond the Tyranny of Testing: Relational Evaluation

· *Anna is in the midst of exam week. She spends hours in memorizing, cramming in the semester's reading, and worrying.*

· *Sean is eleven years old and is in a bad mood. He faces two days of national tests, for which the class has been preparing for two weeks. "Why," he asks, "am I sitting here taking these tests"?*

· *Ron is preparing for college entrance tests. He wants to study art history, but he is frustrated and fearful because he can't get into college unless he makes a high score in math.*

Such are the results of a factory orientation to education. Each of these students is under a microscope – dispassionately observed and judged by others. Their own particular interests, enthusiasms, and skills are irrelevant, and the outcome could determine the direction of their lives. The levels of stress and anxiety have never been greater, and most students view testing and grading as the worst feature of their education. In addition, while assessment is designed to increase learning, its consequences are often the reverse. Students tend to learn only that for which they will be tested, and most of this will be forgotten within three months. The lesson they do learn is the skill of passing tests. Further, teachers will narrow their teaching to what will appear on the test. One "teaches to the test."

While these are among the many critiques of tests and grades, we must also ask about their consequences for relationships, most importantly between students and their teachers, their parents, and their classmates. Does the relational process favored by the assessment tradition energize learning and foster wellbeing? At the outset, the system of assessment is based on a separation of individual units. Students are assessed for their individual performance; each is defined as fundamentally alone, and assessment will rank them in an order of worth. The relation among students is thus a competitive one, with low scores a source of shame and high scores justifying a sense of superiority. Because teachers function as judges in these matters, they may be feared or flattered. Simultaneously teachers are thrust into an alienating posture of surveillance: are students doing their own work, are they cheating, are they applying themselves? Teachers are also assessed, frequently by the scores of their students on national exams. In this case teachers are also confronted with anxiety, and their poorly performing students are a burden. The stage is fully set for degenerative relations.

To be sure, feedback can be very useful in the process of learn-ing. "Does this solution work better than that one?" "What if I move in this direction as opposed to that?" "Can you understand me if I say it this way as opposed to that...?" Learning and feedback walk hand in hand. The critical challenge is finding a viable alternative to the flawed tradition of assessment. How, then, might we approach evaluation from a relational standpoint? Most importantly, what kind of relational process would contribute to learning, curiosity, engagement, and a continuing appreciation of the fruits of learning? Moreover, could such a process enrich the potentials of the relational process itself? Let us shift, then, from assessment to processes of *relational evaluation.*

In this vein, forward-looking educators from around the world have developed practices of evaluation, many of which are congenial with a relational orientation to evaluation. Here are three of the most widely used:

Portfolios. Testing and grading young children have always been controversial. In an increasing number of schools, such assessments are replaced by portfolios. Here students collect materials during the semester for presentation to the teacher at the semester's end. A portfolio might contain evidence of completed tasks, notebooks, drawings, diaries, projects, charts, posters, computer work, and more. They can illustrate the pupils' best work, or any work that the child feels proud of or that demonstrates his/her knowledge and skills. At the semester's end, each student discusses the contents of the portfolio with the teacher, and possibly the parents. The teacher may ask the child what they have enjoyed or found interesting, thus initiating a dialogue with the child. Together they may also explore what the child believes are good demonstrations of his or her learning.

Portfolios have many advantages over tests and grades. They eliminate students' anxiety of being tested, and they give them the opportunity to extend their interests. At the same time, children are invited to reflect on their learning, what they feel is important to learn, and why. Of special importance, the relationship between the child and the teacher shifts from alienation to collaboration. They become partners in learning. Such advantages have also stimulated the development of portfolio practices in secondary school and beyond.

The Learning Review. For secondary schools in the UK, a frequent alternative to grading is the learning review. The learning review invites the student to record their learning activities over the course of a semester or longer. Students may variously be asked to keep a notebook about their interests, their goals, and accomplishments – both inside the class and out. They may document their challenges, and how they overcame various obstacles. Periodically the student meets with the teacher to discuss the review. The review may also be shared and discussed with other students or with parents. There are no letter grades assigned, and no alienating comparisons with other students.

The learning review is especially beneficial in its inviting students to continuously reflect on their learning. One might say that they become researchers into their own learning. Typically, such research draws them into discussion with others about comparative experiences and challenges. This form of generative relating is complemented by the way the learning review shifts the relationship between students and their teachers and parents. A judgmental orientation is replaced by a team effort.

Collaborative Evaluation. Especially at the university level, innovative practices in collaborative evaluation are now thriving. In this case, students provide feedback on each other's work. For example, a student's essay or a project may be shared with two randomly selected classmates, who discuss what they see as the strong points and areas where they feel improvement could be made. Here students are provided a range of perspectives on what counts as good work, along with a sense of support. At the same time, those evaluating the work can learn about a topic while developing ideas about criteria for good work.

These practices all rely on relationships to provide the kind of feedback that enhances interests and enthusiasm to learn. The relational process also prepares the young for positive participation in the relational flow. It should finally be underscored that these alternatives to testing and grading have reverberating consequences for both teaching and curriculum. By eliminating the controlling power of testing and grading, they also liberate teaching practices. No longer are lectures and power-points, for example, necessary to ensure that the lessons are "stamped into the minds" of students. Dialogues, team projects, project learning and so on can be fully implemented. Further, classes would no longer be driven by a standardized curriculum, with everyone learning the same thing at the same time. Curricula can be flexibly attuned to the needs, opportunities, and limits of time and place.

From Classroom to the Communiverse

In partnering with the young to prepare them for participating in positive flow of coordinated action, we must look beyond the school itself –not only to the local community but to one's region, nation, and to the world. It is to the universe of communities – the *communiverse* – to which education should ultimately be relevant. At the local level, schools often move in this direction in their uses of project-based learning. Thus, students may develop projects for improving transportation to the schools, facilitating recycling, or reducing energy costs. Schools can also draw from the talents and resources of those within the community. Exemplary, however, are programs of intergenerational learning that make use of elders' wisdom in the classroom. In one impressive case from an inner-city primary school, elders are invited to join in one-on-one reading with the young students, to share stories and build relationships with the children.[20] The children are mainly from a poor community and greatly benefit from others spending time with them in listening, conversing, and mentoring. At the same time, many of the elders live alone, and are searching for meaningful activities. Both gain in their learning and mutual appreciation. The program has proven so meaningful the elder mentors have spent more than 4,000 volunteer hours with students within a single academic year.

Relations with business organizations can also expand the learning community beyond the walls of the school. Local businesses are often eager to create positive relationships with schools. An impres-

---

20. Bodiford, K. & Whitehouse, P. (2020). Intergenerative Community Building: Intergenerational Relationships for Co creating Flourishing Futures. In S. McNamee, et al. (Eds.) *The Sage Handbook of Social Constructionist Practice*. London: Sage.

sive case in South Africa emerged from the economic and cultural problems faced by many school principals. A *Partners of Possibility* program was created that paired the school leaders with business leaders willing to help the schools.[21] The hope was that the principals' skills and insights would benefit from the business leaders' experiences in running a complex organization. The two leaders would thus collaborate in identifying problems and working on solutions. So meaningful were these meetings that more than 400 business leaders from over 300 organizations partnered with principals over a five-year period. As school leaders later reported, the parents became increasingly engaged in their schools, with an alliance formed between the schools and the community. There was an increase in energy and dedication on both sides.

Expanding the scope of community engagement, consider a case in which an entire country joined in creating an educational program for children. The South American country of Suriname gained its independence from the Netherlands in the 1970s. As educational programs began taking shape, it was also realized that imposing systems of education from outside the country was insensitive to local needs and traditions. Rather than making decisions from the top on these matters, it was asked, what if the nation's people joined the conversation on elementary education? Guided by an appreciative orientation, an extended interview process was initiated.[22] Included were not only teachers and school leaders, but school inspectors, directors of organizations, government officials, students, parents, fishermen, street vendors, farmers, and more. Hundreds of people from around

---

21. Van Rhyn, L. (2016) Vision 2030: How a South African Provocative Proposition is igniting active citizenship and Collaboration. *AI Practitioner*. August issue.
22. Schoenmakers, L. (2014) *Happily different*. Taos Institute: Worldshare Books.

the country participated in discussions in which they shared positive stories about children's development. They discussed available strengths, hopes, beliefs, and enthusiasms. From these discussions an easily accessible book, *I Believe in You!* was assembled. In turn, the book was circulated about the country for further discussion, and ultimately became the foundation for establishing the elementary school system.

There is much more to be said about removing the barriers separating schools from the worlds of which they are a part. In particular, the internet now provides classrooms with portals to learning relationships across the globe. We can move toward a future in which education is equivalent to participating in the global flow of co-creation.

Further Resources

Alexander, R. J. (2006). *Towards dialogic teaching: Rethinking classroom talk*. Cambridge: Dialogos.

Boss, S. & Krauss, J. (2018) *Reinventing project-based learning: Your field guide to real world projects in the digital age*. 3rd International Society for Technology in Education.

Dole, D., Godwin, L. & Moehle, M. (Eds.) (2014) *Exceeding expectations: An anthology of appreciative inquiry stories in education*. Chagrin Falls, OH: Taos Institute Publications.

Dragonas, T. Gergen, K. J., McNamee, S. & Tseliou, E. (Eds.) (2015). *Education as social construction: Contributions to theory, research, and practice*. Taos Institute: WorldShare Books,

Gergen, K.J. & Gill, S. (2020) *Beyond the tyranny of testing: Relational evaluation in education*. New York Oxford University Press.

Hmelo-Silver, C.E., Chinn, C. A., Chan, C., & O'Donnell, A. M. (Eds) (2016) *The international handbook of collaborative learning*. New York: Routledge.

Lewis, R.E. (2020). Lifescaping: Cultivating flourishing school cultures. In S. McNamee, M. M. Gergen, C. Camargo-Borges, & E. F. Rasera (Eds.) *The Sage handbook of social constructionist practice*. (pp. 321-331) London: Sage.

Lund, G.E. (2020). Creating school harmony. In S. McNamee, M. M. Gergen, C. Camargo-Borges, & E. F. Rasera (Eds.) *The Sage Handbook of Social Constructionist Practice*. (pp. 332-342) London: Sage.

Mercer, N., Wegerif, R. & Major, L. (Eds.) (2020) *International handbook on dialogic education*. London: Routledge.

Udvari-solner, A. & Kluth, P.M. (2017) *Joyful learning: Active and collaborative strategies for inclusive classrooms*. 2nd ed. New York: Corwin.

Wagner, T. (2015) *Creating innovators: Making young people who will change the world*. New. York: Scribner.

4. Healthcare: From Causality to Collaboration

I don't want…to define you or confine you…
All I really want to do…is be friends with you.

– Bob Dylan

THE HEALTHCARE PROFESSIONS – BOTH medical and therapeutic – have become major fixtures in today's world. Expenditures on healthcare have accelerated to the point that they can play a major role in a nation's economy. Caregiving is often linked to the suffering of others – to their needs, disappointments, pain, and so on. This is so both in daily life and in the healthcare professions. The present chapter focuses on the relational process within these professions. Why should we do so? To be sure, acts of caring are fundamentally relational, but why should they draw any particular attention? Aren't these professionals simply doing their job? Indeed, but it is this very question that demands our concern.

The relational process within these professions is largely based on the assumption of separation, with the caregiver and the recipient understood as independent or bounded beings. Further, this relationship is largely structured in terms of *cause and effect*. In application, this means that the therapist or doctor takes action to improve the condition of a flawed individual. The former *treats* the latter, or *combats* the disorder. The relationship is fundamentally instrumental: the job of one is solely to fix the other. In machine-like fashion, the causal agent (therapist or doctor) is a certified expert in matters of treatment, follows standardized protocols, focuses specifically and dispassionately on treating the disorder, and is subject to evidence-based assessment.

To be sure, there is much to be said for such an arrangement, particularly in the medical arena. However, in this cause-and-effect process of relating, who or what do the participants become? Here the picture is far from pretty. Wide-ranging study indicates that medical patients often feel like objects – treated impersonally, not listened to, not respected, and not provided enough information to make judgments. Because of their alienated relationship, patients in the United States often respond by suing doctors for malpractice. In addition to their skyrocketing costs for malpractice insurance, medical practitioners often complain of *burnout* – emotional and physical exhaustion. In the case of therapy, many clients similarly feel they are being processed – subjected to protocols that have little to do with their problems, and provided drug prescriptions instead of sensitive understanding. The goal of wellbeing is not well served.

Not surprisingly, such discontent has also fired the spirit of innovation across the healthcare professions. Most importantly, many of these innovations abandon the mechanistic orientation of cause and effect. In its place, we find an increasing focus on healthcare as a relational process, and increasing attention to the implications for healthcare practices. In this chapter we take a look at a range of these innovations in therapeutic and medical practice. While there is much to be said, we focus here on three major ways in which such practices are currently making a difference: in transforming realities, transforming relationships, and expanding the circles of care.

Transforming the Realities of Health and Illness

Within the relational process we create our understandings of the world, what exists, who and what we are, and what is worthwhile. On this account, there are no problems in the world independent of those who define them as problems. For most people, falling from a three-story window would be a grave problem; others might see it as the solution to a problem. A restless student may feel the teacher is boring; for psychiatrists the student is a victim of an attention deficit disorder. These realities are molded in relationships – with colleagues, friends, families, the media, and so on. As therapists and healthcare practitioners increasingly realize, understandings of the world may thus be transformed in the service of relieving suffering. If new understandings are constructed together, lives may change for the better.

Therapy as World-Making

Since its inception in the early 1900s, psychiatric treatment has been guided by a medical model. From this perspective, people's problems in living are defined as *mental* illnesses, and like physical diseases, subject to classification. At present, in the Western world there are almost 400 designated kinds of mental illness. Many are well known to the public, for example, depression, schizophrenia, bi-polarity, and anxiety disorder. When people's problems are defined as "illnesses," it's the therapist's job to provide a "cure." Psychotherapists offer "talking cures" while psychiatrists now turn to "chemical cures." There are many critics of this application of the medical model. Most important for our purposes, however, is criticism of the way people's problems are defined as "illnesses" or "disorders." As those searching for help will learn from their therapists, "I am mentally ill." Whether this form of understanding is useful to people in their daily lives is a significant question. As many critics see it, when everyday problems of living are reconstructed as illnesses, people come to see themselves as personally flawed, socially inferior, and needy – all affecting their relations with others.[23]

Increasingly problematic is the therapist's reliance on pharmaceutical "cures." Following the medical model, it is only natural to "cure illnesses" by biological means. The pharmaceutical industry has boomed as a result, with billions of dollars in sales contributing to the mushrooming of healthcare costs. To illustrate, energetic children didn't know they were "suffering from a mental disorder" until psychiatrists created a diagnostic category for them in the year 2000. In the United States, over one in ten school children are now diagnosed with Attention Deficit Hyperactivity Disorder, and their parents are informed that they may never recover. National healthcare costs for ADHD in the U.S are over 20 billion dollars.[24]

It is in this context that new therapeutic movements have sprung to life. If "mentally ill" is only one way of defining people we find

---

23. Conrad, P. and Barker, K.K. (2010) The social construction of illness: Key insights and policy implications. *Journal of Health and Illness.* 51S: 67-79.
24. US National Library of Medicine www.ncbi.nlm.nih.gov/pmc/articles/PMC1180839/

problematic, then alternative understandings can be generated. What if therapy were envisioned as a relational process in which new and promising realities are created? Perhaps the major movement inspired by such ideas is *narrative therapy*.[25] As reasoned in this case, people understand themselves largely in terms of stories. As multi-beings, we carry with us many stories of our lives, and these stories become central to our self-understanding and relations with others. These are often stories of success and failure, how I won the game or failed to get the job I wanted. In this context, what we call a problem is only so within a particular story. Consider a client who reports, "I was doing well, but then my marriage fell apart, and I started getting bad reports on the quality of my work. Now I am miserable, and I don't feel like going on with life."

As narrative therapists see it, this is only one way of telling a story about oneself, and it is a story that has become so convincing that it invites suicide. In this sense, it is not the client who has a problem; *the problem lies in his embracing a story that defines him as having a problem.* In this case therapy is essentially a conversation that enables clients to *re-story"* themselves in ways that invite more promising ways of going on. What if this story of failure could be replaced, for example, as a valuable road to self-discovery, or a signal of resilience? The therapeutic conversation might enable just such possibilities to take root, and become realized in daily life.

There are many other ways in which therapists work with clients to generate more promising realities. Another prominent idea is that of shifting the focus of the therapeutic conversation. Most people

---

25. White, M., & Epston, D. (1990). *Narrative means to therapeutic ends.* New York: Norton.

come to therapy because they have a problem, and therapeutic conversation typically focuses on the nature and source of the problem. However, if people talk about what they see as their problems, the problems become more central to them, more detailed, concrete, and convincing. If they search their past for why they are suffering, they may begin a long journey into discovering the depth and dimension of their illness. As sometimes said, living with the belief one is mentally ill is sometimes more stressful than the problem initially reported to the therapist. Thus, it is reasoned, we make significant strides by shifting the direction of therapy from "problem talk," to "solution talk."[26] Where do clients want to go with their lives, what would a desirable future look like, and how could they get there? What avenues do they have for moving toward these goals, and who might support them? If the conversation is shifted to the future, to one's visions of what might be possible, new ideas begin to flourish along with a sense of optimism.

In a related vein, many therapists find it useful to shift the focus of conversation away from the clients' sufferings, failings or shortcomings, and to focus instead on their strengths. Recall the discussion in the preceding chapter of strength-based teaching. Such a focus can build client self-confidence, nourish enthusiasm, and encourage a proactive stance toward the future. Many have praised these forms of therapy for the rapid way they can bring about change. As reasoned, the therapeutic process can be brief, because there is no need for the more traditional plumbing of the dark memories of the past.

Innovative therapists are hardly alone in seeing the positive potentials of transforming realities. There are numerous groups in

---

26. DeShazer, S. (1994). *Words were originally magic.* New York: Norton.; O'Hanlon, B. (2000). *Do one thing differently.* New York: W. Morrow.

society that are commonly labeled as mentally ill or disabled. As these groups have increasingly realized, these common labels are social constructions that are limited, harmful, and alienating. By banding together, counter-constructions can be forged, and these may have the power of changing their lives and society at large. One of the most important lessons in transforming such realities emerged in the 1950s in the United States, a time when homosexuality was treated as a mental illness and a crime. Through the concerted efforts of the gay community, law makers, and mental health professionals, homosexuality was removed from the psychiatric list of mental illnesses and from criminal statutes. This liberation of an oppressed minority has sent signals across a broad spectrum of people who have been marginalized by common labeling.

One of the most impressive examples of grass roots resistance to harmful labeling is the *Hearing Voices* movement (www.hearing-voices.org). People who experience voices speaking to them – possibly demanding that they act in destructive ways – have traditionally been labeled schizophrenic. Yet, as an increasingly large number of people ask, why is hearing voices called a disease? They point out that hearing voices is not so uncommon, and indeed many famous people – Socrates, William Blake, Gandhi, and Freud – all managed quite well with their voices. The international hearing voices movement now enables participants to join in collective conversation, trading stories and sharing useful ways of relating to their voices. Also impressive are movements within minorities labeled as *disabled* – for example, the blind, the deaf, the crippled or paraplegic, and so on. They are studied by outsiders, and public policy affecting their lives has largely been out of their hands. Resistance has slowly accumulated, and now the slogan, "nothing about us without us" has generated a broad political movement. By working together, a strong case has been made for representation in decisions affecting their welfare. As many now propose, a neuro-diverse population contributes to the strength of the species.

Meaning and Medicine

Interests in meaning making are increasingly making their way into the field of medicine. Of special significance is the way in which medical professionals are trained to focus almost exclusively on the patient's physical condition. With a concerted focus on diagnosis and cure, little attention is paid to the patient's world of meaning. More specifically, the medical problem is not just a medical problem for the patient and the patient's loved ones. They live in different realities. Where the doctor sees only a malfunctioning heart valve, the patient may live in dread of surgery, life-long scarring, the loss of career standing, becoming an invalid (*not valid*!), the loss of virility, and so on.

Controversies about what counts as physical illness, cure, and health have also been fixtures in the medical field. In today's globalized world such discussions increasingly center on differences among Western, non-Western, and indigenous traditions of understanding. At the same time, it has become increasingly clear that the meaning-making process is related in numerous ways to physical wellbeing. For example, research finds that those who approach old age with an optimistic view of the future are likely to live longer.[27] For those

27. Danner, D. D., Snowdon, D. A., & Friesen, W. V. (2001). Positive emotions in early life and longevity: findings from the nun study. Journal of Personality and Social Psychology, 80, 804-813.

caught up in a life that provokes frequent anger, the lifespan will be shorter. These studies suggest that the medical model may be inadequate to the practice of medicine itself.

One of the most exciting developments in recent years is the emergence of the narrative medicine movement. Spearheaded by Rita Charon,[28] the movement places critical importance on helping medical practitioners listen to the patients' stories. As she proposes, by understanding patients' perspectives more thoroughly, doctors and nurses can do a better job of caring for their patients. When the dialogue between patients and their caregivers is more open, egalitarian, and involving shared views, the care of the patient is improved. As an advanced medical student reported, "It not only makes me a better physician in the sense of being able to listen better and be more compassionate," but, "it also helps you gain a better understanding of who you are as a person." Overall, the narrative approach shifts the provider's orientation from asking "How can I treat this disease?" to the more inclusive question, "How can I help my patient?" Responding to the earlier critique of mechanized healthcare, many see this orientation as building a relationship of mutual trust between patients and their physicians. Training in narrative medicine is now featured in many medical schools.

Transforming Relationships

As proposed, the relational process can transform our realities in the service of well-being. However, from a relational perspective,

---

28. Charon, R. (2006). *Narrative medicine: Honoring the stories of illness*. New York: Oxford University Press.

attention is also drawn to the health-giving potentials of transforming relationships themselves. What forms of relational process best serve healthcare needs? As noted earlier, the traditional cause and effect structures tend to favor mechanistic or depersonalized forms of relating: "we the experts treat you the flawed." Also established is a hierarchy places professionals in the position of power. They are the "knowers" – independent, capable, unblemished – while those being treated are positioned as ignorant, dependent, and incapable. Thus, the scenarios of relating are severely limited and often alienating. At the same time, there is a sea-change taking place across the healthcare professions – both in therapy and medicine. It is a leveling of hierarchy, a diminishing of distance, and a recognition of the enormous power of collaboration.

Therapy: From Authority to Collective Quest

There are many schools of psychotherapy, each based on different assumptions about human functioning, and each offering unique forms of treatment. Such treatments are then applied to those who seek the services. Again, the premise of cause and effect is typically in play, with the therapist aiming to bring about positive change. At the same time, such pre-designed programs can also feel impersonal and programmed, as if the therapist "already knew," for example, that a person's problem stemmed from their childhood, their lack of self-regard, their cognitive habits, and so on. As a counter to this tendency toward mechanization, discussions have increasingly centered on a therapeutic stance of *not knowing*.[29] By this it is meant that

---

29. Anderson, H. & Gehart, D. (Eds). (2007). *Collaborative Therapy: Relationships and Conversations that Make a Difference.* New York: Routledge.

the therapist is not the expert on the clients' lives; the clients know far more about what they are confronting, the complexities of their circumstances, their successes and failures, and so on. A stance of not knowing invites therapists to become learners, to listen with curiosity and to appreciate the client's ways of understanding. Invited, then, is dialogue and co-inquiry. Therapist and client work together to develop a new future for the client. An authority-based orientation is replaced by collaboration.

A collaborative orientation toward practice can take many forms. Rather than following a specific format or treatment program, the primary feature lies in the general disposition of the therapist. The therapist could be characterized as a generous host, welcoming, interested, curious, and engaged. A collaborative orientation has been especially useful for therapists dealing with minority cultures, and navigating the difficult waters of helping families stressed by multiple and simultaneous problems.[30] Listening carefully, appreciatively, and constructively allows flexibility of movement in these challenging situations. Also congenial with the move toward collaboration, are practices of *multi-family therapy*.[31] Many families are distraught, for example, when a teen-age son or daughter is struggling with drug abuse or self-harm. By placing such families together, wisdom, insights, and coping strategies are shared. Families provide mutual support and sometimes humor. Interestingly, while practices of meditation or mindfulness were almost exclusively devoted to the improvement of individuals, attention now turns to their relational potential.[32]

30. Madsen W.C. (2007) Collaborative therapy with multi-stressed families.2nc ed. New York: Guilford.

31. Asen, E. and Scholz, M. (2010) Multi-family Therapy: Concepts and Techniques. London: Routledge.

32. Aristegui, R., Campayo, G. & Barriga, P. (Eds.) (2020) *Relational mindfulness: Fun-*

This shift from hierarchical to collaborative forms of relating has also carried over into psychodiagnostics in an interesting way. Recall here the critique of mental illness diagnosis, and the ways in which it converts challenges in daily life to mental illnesses. At the same time, by suspending the categories altogether, the psychiatric perspective is also eliminated. Why, it is asked, should we silence any relevant tradition of understanding? Perhaps we gain in potentials by expanding the range of interpretations. With such concerns in play, Jaakko Seikkula and his Finnish colleagues developed a radically different alternative to the psychiatric diagnostics: *the open dialogue.*[33] If someone exhibits "psychotic" symptoms a team is created. Joining the therapist might be a social worker, family members, close friends, teachers, and even the troubled individual. There are no secret meetings among the professionals, no ideas or plans that are not revealed to all of those present, and no time limit on how long or how frequently the dialogues might last. All viewpoints are acknowledged, multiple ideas are put into play, and creative lines of action often result. As research indicates, such dialogues reduce the anxiety of the troubled person, increase his/her trust in the proceedings, and lead to a general willingness to follow the suggestions of the group. Interestingly, hospitalizations decrease dramatically, and fewer people are placed on drugs. By participating in a group that works creatively and collaboratively for their well-being, marked improvement ensues.

damentals and applications. New York: Springer.

33. Seikkula, J., & Arnkil, T. (2006). *Dialogic meetings in social networks.* London: Karnac.

Toward Collaborative Medicine

The appreciation of collaborative process is also changing the face of medical care. Like many large institutions, hospitals are primarily organized in the image of a machine. Like machine parts, each professional group is assigned to a specific task, and if each does its job well, the machine should function efficiently. Thus, we have doctors trained as specialists in cardiology, oncology, pediatrics, and so on. There is also a hierarchy in which the nursing staff, orderlies, and other specialties serve the physicians. As is slowly realized, however, there is little coordination among these groups. Yes, information may be formally passed from one specialist to another, and information could move up and down in the hierarchy. But there is little in the way of "understanding from the other's perspective," and little attention to the patient as a whole. During a 4-day hospital stay, a patient might, for example, interact with as many as 50 different employees, each with a specific mission. An elderly neighbor of mine recently reported that because each of her various specialists had prescribed drugs over time, she had reached the point of taking 19 pills a day! Most importantly, because of these mechanized relations, patients are at risk. As research shows, one of the ten top causes of death in the U.S. is "medical error." – ahead of AIDS, breast cancer, or accidents.[34] And, the leading cause of medical error is a lack of coordination among professionals! There are failures to communicate, misunderstandings, ambiguities, and so on. The patient's wellbeing is at stake.

---

34. O'Daniel, M. & and Rosenstein,A.H. (2008) Professional communication and team collaboration. In Hughs, R.G. (Ed.) *Patient safety and quality: An evidenced-based handbook for nurses.* Rockville, Md.: Agency for Healthcare Research and Quality.

As a result of these conditions, there are wide-ranging attempts to create more collaborative relations among practitioners. Rather than everyone doing their own job to the best of their ability, they become participants in a team. *It is the team* that strives for successful outcomes. Insofar as possible, these teams meet together face to face. So much more can be communicated in the tone of voice, through gestures, and through conversational give-and-take than through formal reports. Interestingly, team coordination is not a "natural" activity for professionals. One learns a specialty, but there is little training in generative communication – in listening with appreciation, synthesizing, and improvising.[35] Some professionals can be dominating, others shy, and so on. Recalling the preceding chapter, traditional education is poor preparation for relational participation. However, when coordination is successful, the results of collaboration are inspiring. Not only do medical errors decrease, but there is more effective treatment, improved safety, greater patient and family satisfaction, and higher morale among the staff.

This emphasis on collaborative care has largely focused on relationships among professionals within the system of healthcare. Yet, we may ask, what about the patient and his or her family? As we saw in the case of narrative medicine, they may have important insights to offer about their care. Particularly in the digital age, patients are sometimes more sophisticated about their condition than their doctors. But there is more. One of the most challenging problems in healing physical illnesses is the lack of patient cooperation. They may not take the prescribed medicines, neglect the prescribed diet,

---

35. Boissy, A and Gilligan, T. (Eds.) (2016) *Communication the Cleveland Clinic way: How to drive a relationship centered strategy for superior patient experience*. New York: McGraw-Hill

continue drinking alcohol and smoking, fail to return for check-ups, and so on. All these failures are invited by the causal form of the relationship: doctors cure patients. With sensitivity to the relational process, a promising alternative emerges: why not add the patient and other family members to a *health-care team*? For example, in one collaborative care initiative, a doctor teams up with patients, their families, and the medical staff to "co-create care."[36] A strong emphasis is placed on each participant being responsive to the hopes, needs, and purposes of all the others on the team. As the initiators write, "Our patients are not just patients to us. We become part of each other in a very interesting way… Their needs become our needs, and our needs become their needs… What we really focus on is what matters as people." (p. 252) The sister of one of their patients was to be married. More than anything else, the patient wanted to be there. As they report, "We got him there."

Expanding the Circles of Healthcare

As we have seen, a sensitivity to relational process has stimulated far-reaching innovation among healthcare practitioners. However, the primary focus has been on relational processes *within* healthcare settings – therapy rooms, hospitals, and so on. At the same time, the logics that inform these innovations are scarcely limited to these traditional settings. Human well-being is inherently a relational process, and the possibilities for expanding the circles of participation are as close as the next conversation. Listening, sharing, supporting, and

---

36. Uhlig, P., & Raboin, W. E. (2015). *Field guide to collaborative care: Implementing the future of health care.* Overland Park, KA: Oak

collaborating can all be life-giving wherever practiced. The challenge is to set such processes in motion – from the local to the global spheres.

Consider first the therapeutic potentials. We have already glimpsed grass-roots movements whose aim has been to enhance the well-being of those otherwise labeled as mentally ill or disabled. There are also increasing numbers of community based practices such as Alcoholics Anonymous and other 12-step programs to reduce addiction. All rely for their efficacy on mutually supportive relationships among the afflicted. In the case of so-called disabilities, many forward-looking businesses have begun to think creatively. A disability is only a disability in specific contexts; in other conditions it may be prized. In the dead of night, the blind lead the way for those disabled by their dependency on sight. Thus, businesses locate ways in which to prize the unique contributions that can be made by the blind, the autistic and other exemplars of neuro-diversity.

Is it possible that the broader community could function in a similar, health-giving way? How could the community itself provide mutual support? A Brazilian initiative is inspiring. Marilene Grandesso and her colleagues have developed an *integrative community therapy* approach.[37] Here the attempt is to draw from resources within the community for dealing with the kinds of problems typically reserved for clinics. As reasoned, within the community there are large reservoirs of wisdom, experience, and understanding. In sharing these resources, community members can learn from each other, and simultaneously gain an appreciation of the community

37. Grandesso, M.A. (2020) Integrative community therapy: Creating a communitarian context for generative and transformative conversations. In S. McNamee, et al. (Eds.) *The Sage Handbook of Social Constructionist Practice*. London: Sage.

itself. Thus, community meetings are typically built around a theme related to a particular problem, such as alcohol or substance abuse, discrimination, conflict, or family violence. The individual confronting the chosen problem, is given an opportunity to relate the details while others listen, and subsequently ask questions. An open discussion then follows in which community members offer advice, relate personal stories, offer different perspectives and so on. All learn from the exchanges, and mutual appreciation abounds.

What about the more difficult challenge of the severely disturbed, those often labeled *psychotic*? Typically, such individuals are either placed in institutions or medicated – often for life in both cases. The health-giving potentials of these treatments are minimal. They function more like protective devices, so that the inscrutable and unpredictable among us will not unsettle the comfort of our social norms. What if the relational conditions were different? Rather than protecting the common norms against intrusion, what if the norms were softened in such a way that there was opportunity for developing positive coordination? Swedish therapists have explored just this possibility.[38] In this case individuals who are severely disturbed – who have possibly spent years in mental hospitals – are placed in a calming, nurturing, and supportive environment. A farm can be an ideal setting, and the farm family is trained to be as accepting and non-demanding as possible. Family members go about their daily lives, and "the guest" lives among them. Nothing is required, but the invitation is always open to join in the daily activities on the farm, from chatting or eating together, to helping with chores. Professional

---

38. Håkansson, C. (2009). *Ordinary life therapy: Experiences from a collaborative systemic practice.* Chagrin Falls, OH: Taos Institute Publications.

therapy sessions are provided once a week, primarily to talk about how life is going on. On special occasions the family, therapy staff, and the guest all get together for meals or a party. When the guest feels capable, arrangements are made for moving to an individual apartment where an independent life begins. However, the guests never have to relinquish their relationships with those who have hosted them. Former guests often return to these families for special holidays or vacations, and the bonds are long-lasting. Importantly, the recovery rate for this kind of treatment is high.

Turning to the medical world, movements toward collaboration within communities are few. But, one does find the medical professions increasingly open to voices from outside their circles. Consider medical education. Traditionally such training is devoted to knowledge developed within the scientific community – in fields such as chemistry and biology, and in their application. However, as we saw in the case of narrative medicine, the experience of patients can be an invaluable addition to treatment. The same holds true in the case of training doctors to care for various populations. For example, the elderly have lived a lifetime of experience with both illnesses and physicians. Young physicians could benefit greatly from knowing about their experiences. In this vein, a program was developed at Harvard Medical School in which elderly ex-patients are invited to join a Council of Elders. Their task is to provide advice to medical residents facing challenging cases.[39] Not only do the elders function as teachers, but as collaborators in building a community of resources for dealing with complex medical cases.

39. Katz, A. Conant, L., Inui, T., Baron, D. and Bor, D. (2000). A council of elders: Creating a multi-voiced dialogue in a community of care. *Social Science and Medicine*, 50, 6, 851-860.

A similar move toward integrating outside voices is taking place in medical research. Increasingly, medical researchers begin to see the advantage of listening to the experiences of those who have the illnesses they wish to study. Thus, researchers have enlisted Parkinson's patients, for example, to join in setting research agendas for studying the disease.[40] Moving further into the public realm, researchers at an academic medical center in Boston recruited a dozen youth of color to help them understand the health needs – both medical and therapeutic – existing in the community.[41] The group of teenagers met together with specialists to consider a range of relevant issues. Based on their discussions, they helped to develop and conduct neighborhood surveys. Later, they helped elaborate on the meaning of the findings and think through implications for policies and planning health care delivery. The circles of co-creation expand.

The collaborative movement in healthcare featured in this chapter is far-reaching in its potential. However, there is now the serious challenge of expanding the circle of participation to the global level. The Corona virus pandemic sweeping the globe, killing millions in its wake, was a dramatic wake-up call. People are moving across the globe in steadily increasing numbers. All carry with them microbiotic habitats. At the same time, the degradation of the environment brings with it biological changes of unknown consequence. The world is little prepared for a future in which deadly illnesses may emerge at any time and rapidly place the human species in jeopardy. We shall return to this issue of global collaboration in the final chapter.

---

40. Abma, T. *et al.* (2018) *Participatory research for health and social well-being.* New York: Springer.

41. Sprague, M. *et al.* (2020) Changing the face of healthcare delivery: The importance of youth co-participation. *Health Affairs,* 39: 1776-1782.

Further Resources

Anderson, H. & Gehart, D. (Eds). (2007*). Collaborative therapy: Relationships and conversations that make a difference*. New York: Routledge.

Chadbourne, J. & Silbert, S. (2011). *Healing conversations now: Enhance relationships with elders and dying loved ones.* Chagrin Falls: Taos Institute Publications.

Hedtke, L. (2020). From an individualist to relational model of grief. In S. McNamee, M. M. Gergen, C. Camargo-Borges, & E. F. Rasera (Eds) *The Sage handbook of social constructionist practice.* London: Sage.

Holzman L., & Mendez, R. (Eds). (2003). *Psychological investigations: A clinician's guide to social therapy.* New York: Brunner-Routledge.

Gold, K. (2020). Words matter: Promoting relationality in healthcare through narrative medicine. In S. McNamee, M. M. Gergen, C. Camargo-Borges, & E. F. Rasera (Eds.) *The Sage handbook of social constructionist practice.* London: Sage.

Lock, A. & Strong, T. (Eds.) (2012) *Discursive perspectives in therapeutic practice.* New York: Oxford University Press.

Nepustil, P. (2020). Populating recovery: Mobilizing relational sources for healing addiction. In S. McNamee, M. M. Gergen, C. Camargo-Borges, & E. F. Rasera (Eds.) *The Sage handbook of social constructionist practice.* London: Sage.

Newbury, J. (2013). *Contextualizing care: Relational engagement with/in human service practices.* Chagrin Falls, OH: Taos Institute Publications.

Paré, D. (2013). *The practice of collaborative counseling & psychotherapy: Developing skills in culturally mindful helping.* Los Angeles: Sage.

5. Organizations and the Challenge of Change

In the long history of humankind (and animal kind too) those who learned to collaborate and improvised most effectively have prevailed.

– Charles Darwin

WE ARE IMMERSED IN AN increasingly rapid and globe-spanning movement of ideas, information, people, inventions, opportunities, and values. The challenges posed to organizations – large and small – are enormous. Are contemporary organizations adequate to such challenges? Consider here that the 20th century conception of the organization was based on the image of a solid, machine-like structure. Like schools and hospitals, organizations have been designed to achieve specific goals –manufacturing, banking, military defense, education, and so on. The typical design divides the organization into machine-like parts, with each element assigned a specific function – such as finance, marketing, human resources, and so on in large corporations. In turn, successful functioning depends on the performance of individuals trained or prepared for a specific job. To ensure the overall functioning of the machine, a hierarchy is required. The top-level "runs the machine," with lower-level managers overseeing the various functions, and so on. The major question remains: is this 20th century machine-like organization adequate to 21st century challenges?

To be fair, in a stable world, these "command and control organizations," can be highly effective in organizing large numbers of people to achieve a specific goal. When the conditions are stable, and there are reliable inputs and predictable needs for its products, effective planning can be very useful. But in a world of increasingly rapid and unpredictable change, the traditional organization becomes obsolete. Required are forms of organizing that facilitate rapid and responsive movement within the flow of global change. Flexibility, improvisation, and innovation are essential. A new vision of the organization is vital.

Let us abandon the idea of the organization as a mechanistic structure, and explore its potentials as an ongoing relational process. This idea has indeed captured the attention of many organizational scholars, and emerging from their work is the pivotal metaphor of the *organization as conversation.* Here the focus is on the continuous process of making meaning, and how this process generates understandings of one's identity, one's job, "good work," just compensation, and so on. Motivation, dedication, and the sense of well-being are all dependent on the process of co-constructing meaning. In what follows we explore the potentials of this relational orientation in the effective functioning of organizations in today's fluid worlds. Most importantly, what kinds of organizational practices are now invited? Drawing from innovations already functioning, we touch here on four developments of particular promise.

Unleashing the Potentials of Participation

In a world of rapid and unpredictable change, one of the chief short-comings of the command-and-control organization, is its strangulation of the relational process. Those at the top make all the significant decisions, and their policies and plans are communicated downward through the organization. In effect, "*we* decide and the rest of you listen and obey." Similar to top-down teaching in schools, the potentials of relational process shrink. One major casualty is the quality of decision making. In today's world it is increasingly difficult to predict the outcome of any given decision. At the same time, problems themselves are becoming increasingly complex. Changes in one domain are related to changes in many others. A simple increase in the price of bread may be related not only to its sales, but to employment, the environment, politics and so on. The ripple effects are continuous and unknowable. If deliberation on policies is limited to those on top, so is the range of the knowledge, insight, and opinion brought into the conversation. Increasing the price of bread may be little more than an economic decision for top management. Whereas those who sweep the floors will have much to say about what this means in the lives of the poor.

It is not merely that decisions are less informed in the machine-like organization, but the hierarchical relationship discourages those at the lower levels from thinking about the issues. If all the deliberation is carried out at the top, then everyone else is reduced to the status of a pawn – just obeying orders. What then is the point of noticing, deliberating, and imagining innovations that might otherwise contribute to the organization? What could have been generative conversation about the organization, is often reduced to complaining, derision, or finding fault with those at the top.

If the organization is conversational process, we must *enrich the conversation*. The first challenge in a complex and rapidly changing world is to increase the number and range of voices participating in forming its future. As theorists might say, the organization must become *polyphonic,* or many-voiced. And given the relational basis for creating value, a premium should be placed on generative conversation. In effect, the need is for broad and engaged participation. This may sound idealistic on the one hand, and chaotic on the other. However, a milestone shift in the needed direction occurred with the development in the 1990's of *Appreciative Inquiry*, a practice of organizational change, now shared world-wide.[42]

Consider the traditional organization in which problem solving and planning mainly come from the top down. New policies, plans, or procedures are set in place for everyone to follow. Whether employees understand the reasons for such changes or find them wrong-headed is largely irrelevant. Resistance is frequent, and change may be halting and alienating. It is sometimes said that people care most about what they create. In these terms, Appreciative Inquiry is first a means of expanding the population of creators. But this is just the beginning. Simply adding more voices to the conversation can also bring conflict, confusion, and gamesmanship. The kinds of conversations created by Appreciative Inquiry (AI) not only avoid many of these problems, but invite enthusiasm, a sense of solidarity, and optimism. How is this achieved? Among the key ingredients are:

---

42. Cooperrider, D. and Whitney, D. (2005). *Appreciative Inquiry: A positive revolution in change.* San Francisco: Berrett-Koehler.

· *From Problems to Possibilities* – When conversations center on problems, the result is often an enlargement of the problem and an increasing sense of despair. In contrast, AI conversations shift attention away from the problems to the positive possibilities.

· *Focus on the Valued* – Future planning in organizations is typically tied to material issues such as cost, feasibility, competing options, and so on. Issues of value – "what do we truly value" – are seldom addressed. As often said, materialism – getting and spending – leaves one with a sense of emptiness. Contrastingly, the initial conversations in AI are appreciative. In particular, they focus on what the participants care about, what gives life to their work.

· *Personal Sharing* – Solving organizational problems tends to be impersonal. Logic and evidence are primary. Initial AI conversations enable individuals to share personal stories that illustrate what they appreciate or value about their life in the organization.

· *Practical Planning* – Decisions are usually made by those at the top of an organization. Participants in AI are involved in both the practical planning and in developing ways to see it bear fruit.

Turning to the actual AI practice, careful planning is needed in advance to develop the group's challenge, and to craft the questions that will move them into productive conversation. The conversations themselves are then divided into four phases, often called "the four D's". In the first phase, *Discovery*, participants typically converse in pairs, with their discussion addressing the relevant question of appreciation. For example, if an organization is considering a plan for expansion, the question might focus on what is it about the present functioning of the organization they most value. In discussing the question, each member of the pair is invited to share a personal story to illustrate what they have appreciated most. This is followed by a *Dream* phase in which participants re-convene in the larger group to share their discoveries. With the help of an AI leader, a set of common values is located. As they move into the *Design* phase, participants consider what kinds of plans, policies, or practices would best realize these values in the expansion of the organization. Finally, in a *Deliver* (or *Destiny*) phase, they plan specific changes that should be made and ways in which they can unfold and be monitored.

Appreciative Inquiry has been adapted by organizations – big and small – and throughout the world. It has found its way into corporations, non-profit organizations, schools, churches, communities, and more. Many people also find the orientation useful in everyday family life, or informally at work. Rather than focusing on problems, or finding fault when things to wrong, conversation can be directed toward what *we* value, and how *we* can do more to achieve these goals. Appreciative Inquiry is not just a practice for organizational change; its fundamentals can enrich our ways of living together.

The remarkable success of Appreciative Inquiry has been a game changer in the field of organizational development. In previous decades, changing an organization – improving or shifting its direction – could be costly and time-consuming. This was primarily owing to the vision of the organization as a machine. If changes are to be made in the machine, one seeks expert consultants, research, assessments, and careful deliberation. In contrast, Appreciative Inquiry demonstrates that organizational change can be as fast as the speed of conversation. And with the right kind of dialogue, enthusiasm and solidarity can be ignited. This realization has now given rise to a more general movement: *dialogic organizational development.*[43] Championed here are wide-ranging practices for stimulating organizational change through productive dialogue. Included are practices akin to Appreciative Inquiry, along with forms of conversation that can disrupt taken-for-granted assumptions, generate new and novel ways of going on, and create useful narratives for facing the future. The vistas of possibility are unlimited.

Collaboration and Creativity

When organizational members are alert, engaged, and communicating, the organization is prepared for action. Yet, active participation does not take us far enough. There remains the crucial challenge of collaborating, of working together to solve problems, making complex decisions, moving in new directions, and so on. This can mean working with those who have different skills, perspectives, and values, and who may live in different part of the world. So important is the capacity to collaborate in the fast-moving world of today, that organizations must *"collaborate or perish,"* as one commentator has put it.[44] Here we consider two significant routes to enhancing collaboration, and an illustration of their potentials.

43. Bushe, G.R. & Marshak, R.J. (Eds) (2015) *Dialogic organizational development.* San Francisco: Berrett-Koehler.
44. Bratton, W. & Tumin, Z. (2012) *Collaborate or perish: Reaching across boundaries in a networked world.* New York: Random House.

Collaborative Technologies

One outcome of the mechanical vision of the organization was its minimalist approach to communication. On this view, if each unit in the organization carries out its task as designed, the entire system should run smoothly. The function of communication, then, is to transfer information in the service of effective functioning. Everything else is irrelevant or possibly counter-productive. Yet, in the digital world of rapid change, with the demand for continuous modification and innovation, the minimalist approach is no longer serviceable. Units can no longer survive on information alone. Primary are needs for clarifying, speculating, improvising, and so on – all in the service of collaboration.

This shift toward collaboration has benefitted dramatically from the mushrooming development of digital technologies. Here we find sources for instantaneous collaboration around the globe, 24/7. These technologies have always been effective in transferring information. However, as they have become increasingly effective in carrying visual information, interchange begins to approximate face-to-face dialogue. This enrichment of the process cannot be over-estimated. At the outset, such dialogue allows for continuous clarification in what is being communicated. A nod of the head, a puzzled brow, or a quick question may all contribute to understanding. Non-verbal expressions, such as tone of voice and facial expressions may signal a speaker's doubts or confidence in an opinion, or the importance of what is being said. Of unique significance, shared laughter is made possible. As they say, "laughter is the shortest distance between two people."

Innovations in communication technology are continuously

improving, but an illustration of the potential is useful. In this case, a Scandinavian organization had grown sufficiently large that coordination across the various departments and subsidiaries had become unwieldy. Employees across the spectrum didn't know each other, mutual understanding was lacking, and bringing new ideas into practice was difficult. Through video technology, systematic meetings were arranged that linked various departments and subsidiaries together with top management. With full visual access to each other, discussions ranged widely, depending on needs and circumstances. As groups became familiar with each other, dialogue became increasingly relaxed and open. In the making was a fund of good will and understanding, both essential for moving forward in ambiguous and ever-changing circumstances.

Scaffolding Dialogue

Bringing people together for collaborative conversation has promising potentials, but collaborative conversation is not a natural act. As explored in Chapter 3, our educational systems prepare us poorly in the arts of collaboration. Classrooms train young students to accept authority, and older students to defend their own positions and criticize competitors. Neither of these makes a promising contribution to collaboration. We are little prepared to expand and elaborate others' ideas, balance and blend multiple positions, or play with ideas and images – all essential to collaborating across divides of meaning. Organizations increasingly see how essential these "soft skills" are for thriving in a multi-cultural world. Increasingly prevalent are manuals on how to work well with others. However, the gap between reading about what one *should do*, and actually doing it can be huge.

In the thick of action, one quickly forgets that, "I should manage my emotions," "stay on track" or "give positive feedback."

For many organizations this has meant adding dialogic skills to management training. However, a second and highly promising route to constructive dialogue is through scaffolding. Rather than relying on shaky skills of relating, or an organizational structure, the attempt is to establish a conversational scaffold that invites collaboration. One of the earliest and most successful scaffoldings of this kind was designed to improve group decision making.[45] To avoid the corrosive effects of hierarchy and competition, the decision-making process is broken into six different types of conversation. In each part, participants "put on a different conversational hat." Thus, in a White Hat phase everyone is invited to share information relevant to the decision; in a Yellow Hat period they are asked to share optimism about the decision they are favoring. Then, in a Black Hat period they can speak out on what they see as the problems or dangers; in a Red Hat conversation, participants speak more subjectively – about their feelings, hunches, and intuitions; in the Green Hat period they are free to imagine alternatives; and during a Blue Hat period, participants reflect on their dialogue itself – how the conversation went, and what they had accomplished. This practice is especially attractive, as it frees the participants from the usual demands of being consistent; they can speak both for and against the same idea. As well, the process vastly increases the range of ideas and sentiments brought to bear in making a decision.

As conversation has replaced the machine metaphor of the organization, scaffolded dialogues have multiplied. Different clusters of

45. DeBono E. (1985) *Six thinking hats*. Boston: Little Brown.

practices have emerged, designed for different kinds of challenges and conditions. For example, a large group of practices has been identified as *liberating structures*. These are structured forms of dialogue that are mainly designed to energize a group so it can reach its potential.[46] The structured dialogues may involve mutual interviewing, role playing, narrative sharing, and so on. To illustrate, in the *Wise Crowds* practice, participants in a small group take turns presenting a personal challenge they are facing in the organization. The listeners in each case, then serve as consultants. They may ask question to clarify, share similar problems, and offer helpful and supportive advice. The participants personally benefit from hearing the multiple viewpoints, and the practice builds mutual trust, confidence, and useful knowledge about life in the organization. Especially stimulating – and full of fun – is a practice called *TRIZ*. In this case the participants may be working on a project together. At some point they pause and share ideas on how they could best achieve *the worst possible results* with their project. Much is learned in the irony. Each of these structured practices may be adapted to given conditions, or modified as needed. In principle, there is no limit to developing such scaffolded practices. Indeed, as a given practice becomes repetitive, it often loses its vitality for the participants.

Creativity by Design

As suggested, two of the major challenges for the future vitality of organizations are collaboration and creativity. The capacity to bring multiple voices into coordination and to respond to continu-

---

46. Lipmanowicz, H., & McCandless, K. (2013). *The surprising power of liberating structures: Simple rules to unleash a culture of innovation.* Seattle: Liberating Structures Press.

ous change with creative action are essential. Both these challenges are addressed in one of the most influential movements of the times: *design thinking*. Realizing the limits of the traditional view of creativity as lodged in the heads of single individuals, the emphasis is placed on creativity as a group process. If the right kind of dialogue is set in motion, creative outcomes are likely. There are many approaches to the "right kind of dialogue" for creativity, but most share a similar logic. Given a desirable goal – such as a new product – a relevant design team is organized. Here it is important to include individuals who differ in their areas of expertise. The dialogue itself is often divided into five phases:

Discover. The team first inquiry into the opinions of those who might be affected by the innovation. For example, if it were a new mousetrap, what do people think of their present mousetraps, their assets and shortcomings; what might they hope for? Here the team tries to understand the situation from the perspective of the potential users.

Define. Given the information collected in the first phase, how is it to be interpreted? What does this information mean in terms of the design? By scanning results and sharing opinions the team might see, for example, that people want traps that are cheap, re-usable, and humane.

Imagine. The group sets out to brainstorm possible designs. Inspired by each other, the imaginations may soar. They might ask whether an actual trap is needed; perhaps there are scents that are noxious to mice but undetected by humans? In the end, the team selects what they feel is a feasible and promising possibility.

Prototype. The next challenge is to draw up a specific design, or prototype of the chosen possibility. What would it look like, what shape and size would it have, and so on. The prototype then becomes the basis for an actual model.

Test. Finally the model is put to the test. What is the experience of the consumer, for example? Is it superior to what currently exists? Where does it fall short?

This shift toward collective creativity now springs from the corporate world, and into public use. Forward-looking policy makers see it as a possible route to solving societal problems.[47] One could design and test alternatives to party politics, or majority rule. The potentials are far-reaching.

Relational Leading

Increasing active participation and facilitating collaboration are critical ingredients for a viable organization. However, there remains the issue of leadership. With the vibrant dynamics of participation and collaboration, how are we to conceptualize leadership? Traditional ideas of organizational leadership center on the individual. Good leaders are contrasted with bad leaders in terms of individual traits – such as courage, integrity, humility, and ability to inspire. In today's machine-like organizations, the leader should manage the machine's functioning and aim for high output. From a relational perspective, the emphasis on the individual leader is misplaced; one cannot inspire or manage alone. We become sensitive instead to the flow of coordi-

---

47. Hassan, Z. (2014) *The social labs revolution: A new approach to solving our most complex challenges*. San Francisco: Barrett-Koehler.

nation. In this case one may see the leader as *actively participating in the flow, so as to enrich its potentials.*

A shift toward a relational concept of leading is increasingly evident in contemporary writings on leadership. Concepts and practices of *distributed leadership, servant leadership, humble leadership, collaborative leadership, co-active leadership*, and *team leadership*, are widely circulated. Here the emphasis shifts from the leaders' individual traits to their role in processes of collaboration, empowering, dialogue, horizontal decision-making, sharing responsibilities, networking, continuous learning, and enhancing connection. In effect, there is a deep and pervasive concern with the process of relating. We may speak more inclusively of *relational leading.*

Theoretically there is no principled reason that organizations should have designated leaders – individuals who serve as CEOs, presidents, captains, commanders etc. Whatever the outcome the organization will depend on the relational process. However, most organizations in the world today are structured hierarchically, with a single individual placed at the top. Those who occupy such roles are in a unique position. Unlike others, they are usually positioned to initiate action – to invite others into a way of relating. There is much to say on this topic, but here we focus on two prominent activities:

Coordinating the Coordinations: Toward Collective Intelligence

Rather than making decisions for others to follow, relational leading should first be concerned with processes of coordination. Most obviously, this would mean facilitating the kind of engaged participation just discussed. Especially in larger organizations this means that multiple "conversations" will be set in motion. Here a new and critical challenge emerges: *coordinating the coordinations*. Do these many "conversations" flow together as a coherent whole? This has been a problem for machine-like organizations. As we saw, such organizations are usually divided into sub-units, each with a specific function (operations, finance, human resources, etc.). And, as discussed in Chapter 2, as groups are formed, they develop their own particular understandings of the real, the rational and the good. Thus, within a group, the forms of coordination may be healthy and humming. However, the realities and values created within any given group tend to create barriers between *us* and *them*, between "our good ideas" and "their poor judgment." Thus, for example, within the organization's marketing wing, the shared goals and reasoning may be quite different from the production or finance wings. The challenge of leading thus lies in coordinating these potentially diverse worlds.

There are no perfect practices of coordinating across diverse groups in an organization. In the machine-like organization this was typically accomplished through top-level meetings among heads of various units. However, those at the top of the hierarchy are limited by the realities that they themselves have constructed. Many organizations improve coordination through electronic networks – keeping everyone "in the loop." But success much depends on whether these networks simply pass on information, or enable sensitive collaboration. There are formal means of assessing the degree of coordination among units of an organization.[48] This enables leaders to locate com-

---

48. Gittell, J.H. (2009) *High performance healthcare: Using the power of relationships to achieve greater efficiency and resilience*. New York: McGraw Hill.

munication gaps that need attention. But how the units are brought together still remains open. Our previous discussions of facilitating generative participation and collaboration are relevant. Such moves can facilitate sensitive coordination throughout an organization. Yet there are time constraints and dialogic capacities to consider. Continuing creativity is needed.

A striking case of coordinating coordinations is supplied by no less than the military establishment. The military services are usually seen as icons of the top-down, mechanistic form of organization. Those in command dictate both strategy and tactics, and obedience to their orders is absolute. Orders should be obeyed, even if they seem wrong-headed or immoral. Yet, as military leaders have begun to realize, conflicts are becoming increasingly VUCA, that is, *volatile, uncertain, complex and ambiguous.* Under these conditions decision making is extremely difficult. The circumstances are ever-changing, and decisions have life-or-death consequences. How is a rational decision possible? Faced with this dilemma, a General in the US Special Operations Command developed a *team of teams* approach to decision making in combat.[49] In this case, decision making was distributed across the units in the field. Each unit was considered a semi-autonomous team – responsible for taking account of the particular conditions in which it found itself, and deliberating on the wisest course of action. However, each team was also challenged to coordinate with other teams and with the command unit. By exchanging information and opinions, the collaborating teams could function as a single team. While few organizations confront such strenuous

---

49. McChrystal, S. (2015) *Team of teams: New rules of engagement for a complex world.* New York: Penguin.

conditions, the team of teams metaphor may be widely applied.

It is just here that many organizational specialists find it useful to think in terms of *collective intelligence*. We usually consider intelligence to be the property of single individuals; the entire tradition of measuring intelligence is based on this assumption. In this case, however, we are invited to consider the degree to which a collective practice yields intelligent decisions. This is largely a matter of the coordination of coordinations. Each sub-group could make intelligent decisions, but the relations among them could lead to a failure of the whole. To illustrate, within a democracy, there may be a high degree of coordination *within* various political parties. However, if the parties are fundamentally opposed, and are persistently antagonistic in making policy decisions, collective intelligence is threatened. Degenerative dialogue is a birthplace for collective disaster.

Beyond Efficacy: Well-being and the World

This chapter has been almost exclusively focused on the ways in which a relational approach to organizations is essential to their continuing viability. In effect, the discussion has placed its value primarily on the efficacy of the organization. In this final section we must expand the horizon of value to consider human well-being – both within the organization and the world more generally. Perfect coordination within an organization does not necessarily contribute to the well-being of the participants. Assembly line workers can be robotically coordinated, but their wellbeing remains a question.

Here it is useful to consider how relational well-being is achieved through the kinds of practices advanced in the present chapter. For example, when workers actively participate in making decisions, issues of their well-being will be inescapably near. Questions of equity, working conditions, family well-being and so on will find their expression. Further, a practice such as Appreciative Inquiry is far more than a process of collective decision making. As participants share personally meaningful stories, they become caring and empathic listeners. In the case of scaffolding dialogues, the Wise Crowds practice does more than providing advice from multiple perspectives. Enhanced are relations of trust and gratitude. Many dialogic practices can be effective in drawing in minority voices, creating mutual understanding, and dissolving power relations. In the team of teams approach, the result is often the creation of mutual respect.

Continuing innovation is required. Consider for example, the traditional practice of the *performance review*, the periodic assessment of employees' work performance. Much like examinations in schools (Chapter. 3), the assessment is a source of significant anxiety. It defines one as an object under inspection by a superior, and one's adequacy and sense of belonging are thrust into question. The review also communicates to employees that they are competing with each other for advancement in the hierarchy. The result is again a distancing among colleagues, with each attempting to make sure they look better than their mates. In sum, the traditional performance review undermines well-being.[50]

In the same way that educators are experimenting with alternatives to school assessment, so are organizations seeking alternatives to the review. Emerging are multiple efforts to recast the performance

---

50. Culbert, S.A. (2010) *Get Rid of the Performance Review.* New York: Business Plus.

review as a dialogic process. While dialogues can be more sensitive to issues of well-being, the subject/object relationship typically remains in place. Most inspiring here are dialogic practices that shift the focus away from the individual's performance to the relational process in which the individual functions. Thus, for example, rather than inquiring into the employee's strengths and shortcomings, the dialogue centers on such questions as: "How are *we* functioning; what are the strengths in the way *we* work together; what could *we* improve in this process?" Fear and alienation are replaced with a sense of solidarity, and issues of coordination becomes central.

Positive Participation in the Global Flow

If organizations are akin to conversations, there is no boundary between inside and outside. Conversations move across the thresholds, to include the local community and beyond. We must then consider the wellbeing of the broader world of which the organization is a part. There is much to be said on these matters, including for example, relations with the families of employees, the community, with other organizations, and the government.

This is also a context in which the assumption of separate entities has been blinding. The "me first" orientation discussed in Chapter 1 has become an accepted way of life. Particularly in the business world, primary attention is paid to the organization's own wellbeing, and particularly its economic "bottom line." Are *we* prospering?" This self-serving orientation is further intensified with the expansion of neoliberal policies in the West, and their prizing of economic competition. From a relational perspective these views are not only shortsighted, but ultimately dangerous. They are short-sighted, as no organization stands independent of the broader relational process of which it is a part. When the relational process is configured as an economic competition, its ultimate direction is degenerative. The winners become larger and more powerful, while the losers die away. The blossoming of global chain stores, and the resulting disappearance of family-owned shops is only one example. But the devastation is more lethal in this case. The demand for ever-increasing profits has meant that the environment is also among the losers. In the competitive war of all against all, little will ultimately remain standing.

This is scarcely a new issue, and the search continues for ways in which organizations can contribute to a sustainable future. In many nations, the most obvious route to sustainability is through transactional relationships. If organizations make a profit, they should pay back a certain proportion to the society. Taxation is the obvious route in this case, with funds supporting the larger infrastructure (e.g. sanitation, roads, security). However, organizations are much like individuals in their approach to taxes. Taxes are an expense, and the attempt is to pay as little as possible. Society remains an inconvenient burden. More publicly spirited businesses turn to benevolent relationships – voluntarily contributing to charities of many kinds. Yet, while charity does make a significant contribution to the broader world, its significance remains dependent on the continuing good will of the organizations. As critics also suggest, while offering useful bandages, charities fail to treat the sources of suffering – such as systemic poverty or racial prejudice.

Needless to say, reconfiguring the relational process remains a vital challenge for the future. We shall return to this issue in the following chapter. But let us close here with one energizing innovation:

the Business as an Agent for World Benefit initiative.[51] Their aim is to support and stimulate the development of businesses with what may be viewed as a triple bottom line: economic viability, human well-being, and environmental flourishing. Every year "Flourish Prizes" are awarded to companies that exemplify these ideals. For example, among the winners is the AeroFarms company, a business that develops innovative methods of farming. Their particular interest is in producing high quality vegetables, with less water consumption, no pesticides, and higher yields. They also provide education in using and developing these innovations. A second winner, LuminAID creates solar-powered lights that are convenient and affordable. The lights are especially useful in impoverished nations with little electrical power, or those hit by a natural disaster. These renewable light sources are now used in 100 countries around the world. Organizational well-being and global well-being now converge.

---

51. https://weatherhead.case.edu/centers/fowler/

Further Resources

Barrett, F. (2012). *Yes to the mess: Surprising leadership lessons from jazz.* Cambridge: Harvard Business Review Press.

Belden-Charles, G., Willis, M., & Lee, J. (2020). Designing relationally responsive Organizations. In S. McNamee, M. M. Gergen, C. Camargo-Borges, & E. F. Rasera (Eds.) *The Sage handbook of social constructionist practice.* London: Sage.

Bushe, G. & Marshak, R. (Eds.) (2015). *Dialogic organization development: The theory and practice of transformational change.* Noida: Berrett-Koehler Publishers, Inc.

Coleman, D. &. and Levine, S. (2008) *Collaboration 2.0: Technology and best practices for collaboration in Web 2.0 world.* Cupertino, CA: Happy About Books

Gaynor, G. (2002). *Innovation by design: What it takes to keep your company on the cutting edge.* New York: AMACOM.

Haslebo, G. and Haslebo, M.L. (2012). *Practicing relational ethics in organizations.* Chagrin Falls, OH: Taos Institute Publications.

Hernes, T. (2014) *A process theory of organization.* New York: Oxford University Press.

Hersted, L. & Gergen, K.J. (2013). *Relational leading: Practices for dialogically based collaboration.* Chagrin Falls, OH: Taos Institute Publications.

Hornstrup, C., Loehr-Petersen, J., Madsen, J. G., Johansen, T., & Jensen, A. V. (2012). *Developing relational leadership: Resources for developing reflexive organizational practices.* Chagrin Falls: Taos Institute Publications.

Kaner, S., et al. (2014). *Facilitator's guide to participatory decision making.* San Francisco: Jossey-Bass.

Madsen, C.O., Larsen M.V., Hersted, L. & Rasmussen, J.G. (2018) *Relational research and organizational studies.* London: Routledge

Sawyer, K. (2007) *Group genius: The creative power of collaboration.* New York: Basic Books.

Uhl-Bien, M. & Ospina, S. (Eds.) (2012). *Advancing relational leadership theory: A Dialogue among perspectives.* Charlotte NC Informational Age.

Verheijen, L., et al. (2020). *Appreciative Inquiry as a daily leadership practice.* Chagrin Falls OH: Taos Institute Publications.

6. Conflict, Control, and the Relational Imperative

*We are tied together in the single garment
of destiny, caught in an inescapable
network of mutuality. And whatever affects
one directly affects all indirectly.*

– Martin Luther King, Jr.

IN SHIFTING THE FOCUS FROM individuals to relational process, we invite life-giving practices in education, healthcare, and organizational life. Such practices are vital in a world of rapid and globe-spanning change. These were among the conclusions drawn from the last three chapters. Such innovations inspire hope and confidence in our potential to co-create more positive futures. Yet, relational process does not in itself guarantee any of these outcomes. Indeed, the forms of mechanization and dehumanization pervading our schools, businesses, and healthcare systems are themselves co-created. And too, the degenerative and downward spirals of bullying, political rancor, racial oppression, and warfare are the unthinking byproducts of relational coordination.

Thus, the question is not whether our ways of life depend on relational process, but do our existing ways of relating foster human and environmental well-being? For whom are they beneficial, who suffers, and how is planetary life affected? Such questions must be continuously addressed, as world conditions change at a rapid rate. Yesterday's "good ideas" can be today's afflictions. Further, our technologies now mean that any action may instantaneously "go global." What, then, is an optimal form of life; for whom, and for how long will it remain so? In a world of plural realities and values, we should be wary of "solid" answers to such questions, and celebrate our continuing search together.

This final chapter is thus devoted to a fundamental tension of continuing concern. One might variously see this as a tension between chaos and control, freedom and order, or fragmentation and unity. However, I will approach the issue here in terms of the tension between peace and conflict. On the one hand, this will allow us to bring together some of the conceptual and practical themes from the preceding chapters. At the same time, it will open the door to one of the today's most pressing issues: governance. Longstanding practices of governing are not only losing their efficacy; they are becoming threats to global well-being. A relational orientation is imperative.

Peace and Conflict: The Delicate Balance

Broadly speaking, there will always be two closely related processes at work in the social world. First, there is a movement toward increased coordination – toward a common agreement, a valued way of life, or in short, a state of peace. In most spheres of life, we strive toward harmonious coordination. As agreeable forms of coordination develop, a reliable way of life may develop – our way, a good way, a tradition. We may also place names on these ways of life – friendship, the Smith family, our community, the Argo Company, and so on. Clusters of coordination thus become identified as units. As these centers of coordination develop, so are tendencies invited to sustain, protect, honor, grow, and enrich them.

These same familiar and comforting tendencies invariably encounter obstacles – disruptions, interference, or threats. From family gatherings rejected by a teenage daughter, a company policy resisted by a disgruntled worker, or an international peace agreement scrapped by a rogue government. Harmony gives way to discord. Most importantly, these disruptions did not emerge from nowhere. They are all intelligible actions *within* a sphere of relating – the daughter's relations with friends, the worker with his family, the errant government sensing threat. They too are the outcomes of coordinated activity, people attempting to build, sustain, or defend a way of life. Ironically, as people everywhere create agreeable realities, rationalities, and moralities, they simultaneously plant the seeds of discord. Wherever there is a valued way of life, there is simultaneously generated an outside, a lesser valued, or a threat to the good. Every valued way of life stands in potential conflict with other ways of life. From a relational perspective, conflict is not then an unusual deviation from the normal; it is a common outcome of peoples everywhere moving toward more satisfying forms of coordination.

The implications are significant. First, we should not presume that conflict is inherently a deviation from peace. Peace and conflict walk hand in hand – a more or less a natural outcome of co-creating ways of life. Further, conflict harbors positive potential. For one, when there is conflict, there are multiple goods in play – plural values emerging from different traditions of meaning making. In this sense, conflict presents an opportunity for learning. "What do they find good that we are missing?" "How can we share in such a way that we are all enriched?" Finally, when conditions are entirely peaceful, caution is warranted. This may be a sign of systemic injustice, where people have ceased to reflect on who gains and who loses by the accepted conditions. Worse still, a perfect peace may hide perfect oppression. In many contexts a challenge to the status quo is a lethal risk.

As we see, the human challenge is not that of achieving an everlasting and satisfying peace on earth. As Leonard Cohen sang, "There's a crack in everything; that's how the light gets in." Instead, the initial challenge is to generate the means by which conflicting ways of life do not destroy the possibility for co-creating meaning altogether. We are reaching a point in history where mutual annihilation is on the horizon. The second challenge is more inspiring: How can we replace the slide into corrosive conflict with more inclusive and flourishing ways of life?

Conflict and Co-Creation: A Relational Approach

In responding to these critical challenges, let's first consider the kinds of practices we inherit from the past? What relational forms have we human beings co-created for dealing with conflict? Scanning the centuries, three major traditions stand out. The most common and most primitive means of treating those who disagree or interfere is *punishment*. Physically this may mean anything from beating, flogging, imprisonment, or torture to elimination. All these options remain with us today, and the list continues to expand – from shunning to shaming to cyber-warfare.

As a second and preferred alternative to punishment, we also inherit forms of *bargaining.* Here, the conflicting parties make trades that will allow each to have a portion of what they value. Parents often bargain with their children in much the same way that management bargains with unions, and nations negotiate their way out of lethally threatening situations. Coming into prominence in the 20th century is a third major approach to resolving conflict: *logical argument.* Mainly due to advances in science, it seemed reasonable to assume that when there are conflicting points of view, a logical assessment of the facts would point the way to a just solution. Courtroom procedures – where judgments should depend on reasoning and evidence – are illustrative.

From a relational standpoint, none of these approaches holds strong promise for the future. Even when there are seemingly peaceful solutions, each of them sustains the assumption of separated units – a *me vs. you,* or an *us vs. them.* One can create peace by punishing or imprisoning the disagreeable, but alienation, suspicion, fear, and resistance will remain. In the case of bargaining, the participants may reach a satisfactory "deal," but they will each remain fundamentally invested in their own gain. Peace will prevail only so long as the terms of the bargain remain useful to both parties.

As for rational arguments, satisfactory solutions can be reached only so long as all parties agree on the premises. For example, a fact is a fact only so long as there is agreement on assumptions. We may commonly agree that "the traffic light was red," while a psychologist will tell us that we are mistaken, "Color is not a property of the world, but of light reflected on the retina." In the same way, the abortion debate cannot be solved by recourse to facts, because the conflicting parties cannot agree on whether a fertilized egg is a human being. That question cannot be solved by reason and observation. Further, judges and juries in the courtroom are moved not only by logic and facts but also by their views on fairness, values, and morality. "Good arguments" are born within traditions of relating.

Relational Forms for Peace Building

Although it seems "just natural" to use force, to bargain, or argue, we should not forget that these are human inventions. None of them are required; all are optional. Most importantly, we can create new relational forms. It is thus, for example, that many legal battles have been avoided by the invention of mediation. Mediation practices are based on the assumption that for many conflicts, a third-party mediator can help in locating less contentious means of settling the differences. From a relational perspective, the questions of communication theorist Barnett Pearce are on target:

- What are we making together?
- How are we making it?
- What are we becoming as we make this?
- How can we make better social worlds?[52]

While peace building may be our goal –*what* we wish to achieve – the question of *how* we do it together is crucial. This is essentially the invitation to create forms or practices of relating. It is within this process that the participants take on identities and characteristics.

---

52. Pearce, B, (2007) *Making social worlds: A communication perspective*. Oxford: Blackwell. p. 53

A practice that creates the participants as winners and losers may achieve peace, but at the possible cost of lasting alienation. With caring attention to the relational practice, we may indeed create better social worlds.

Preceding chapters have demonstrated how the creation of new relational practices has enhanced the worlds of education, healthcare, and organizational life. Because of the centrality of conflict and its consequences in our lives, the search for new ways of going on has been vigorous. While several resources are included at the chapter's end, it is useful here to consider some of the logics that have been central to innovations in a relational vein. Bringing these into focus will also help in knitting together central themes in the earlier chapters. Here we focus on five specific logics and their practical realizations:

Discouraging Degenerative Dances: "Let's not go there." When conflict is understood in terms of antagonism – with one party against another – we invite a dialogue of mutual disparagement. That is, participants will find it normal to blame, criticize, or verbally abuse each other. As outlined in Chapter 2, such aggressive moves in a conversation invite counter-attack; and from there, a degenerative slide into antagonism and separation. Realizing the danger of this relational dance, innovators create forms of dialogue that either inhibit or discourage degenerative scenarios. This is accomplished in two major ways. The indirect route is commonplace in daily life: we avoid talking about issues over which they disagree. We understand that to "go there" could bring bitterness and the end of a friendship. In peacebuilding practices, this often means avoiding direct confrontation with issue about which there is disagreement – at least for a time – and inviting participants into more congenial activities. This could mean, for example:

- Personal introductions in which participants talk about their family lives or personal history.
- Sharing a meal together.
- Collaborating on a joint project.
- Directing the conversation to the kinds of daily challenges they face.

Innovators have also developed more direct means of inhibiting the slide into alienation. For example, this can be accomplished by:

- Restricting participants to speaking about themselves (*my* perception of the situation, feelings, desires, motives, etc.), as opposed to characterizing the other as the cause of the problem. This tends to avoid the scenario of fault-finding ("what *you* did!"), and mutual blame.
- Restricting conversation to concrete cases, as opposed to abstract principles ("my right to do this"). This avoids the endless and insoluble arguments about abstract rights, duties, or ethical principles.

Inviting Generative Scenarios. As proposed, our ways of making sense together are like dances. They are patterns of collaborative action that often become normalized. When one is verbally attacked, it is "just natural" to counter-attack. And, like dances, they are open to improvisation and invention. Introducing a new move into the ongoing dance disrupts the "natural" pattern and invites the other into innovation. For example, the Christian ideal of "turning the other cheek," in response to another's attack, can disrupt the endless cycle of revenge and counter revenge. Productive disruptions in normal scenarios of antagonism are useful in peacebuilding. Consider for example:

· Proposing that the conflict is an opportunity for growth in understanding.

· Drawing attention to the interchange itself. For example," Do we really want to treat each other like this?" "Can we stop for a moment and ask ourselves if there isn't a better way to solve this problem?"

In addition to disrupting the commonplace, peacebuilders have also opened the door to creating new relational scenarios. Perhaps the most visible of these are emerging in the dynamic field of *restorative justice*. Keeping the peace through systems of justice, usually relies on punishment – from scolding rowdy children, expelling the bully from school, to imprisoning lawbreakers. Such punitive forms of relational process are both primitive and alienating for all concerned. Restorative justice programs are devoted to repairing relationships. They attempt to reconcile the harm doers with the victims, and integrate the harm doer back into the community. An extended scenario, in this case, might include the following steps:

· *Encounter*. Those who have suffered because of the offender's actions, talk about the effects of these actions on their lives – their misery, others who have suffered, and so on. In listening to these stories, the offender frequently empathizes with the victim.

· *Making amends*. The offender accepts responsibility for his or her actions, and apologizes.

· *Reintegration*. The victims and the offender discuss how they can go on together; plans are made for reintegrating the offender into the community.

There are many variations in restorative justice practices, and such programs have been enormously successful in resolving conflict in schools and reintegrating criminal offenders into community life. As often found, these programs can create a sense of community solidarity. Training programs now spring up in schools and cities across the lands.

Creating New Realities: "It is not what we thought." In most conflict situations, the opposing parties bring to the table differing understandings of the world. Each will understand the world in a way that justifies their position. However, if these differing orientations are born within a relational process, they can be changed through the same means. As we saw in Chapter 3, many schools of therapy have made the reconstruction of reality a centerpiece of practice. Therapy is devoted to nurturing more promising forms of understanding self and the world.

In peacebuilding, this line of reasoning has led to the development of *narrative mediation*. Understandings of the world are represented in narratives, or stories about "what led to what." In this sense, protagonists each bring to the table a self-justifying story – "this is why I am right, and you are wrong."[53] With sensitive probing of these accounts, however, the mediator locates instances or experiences that don't quite fit the story. "Well, there was this time when you were right…" or "yes, I guess I am partially to blame for this…" In discussing these further, the dominant story is destabilized, and a scaffold is erected for developing alternative narratives. With the help of the mediator, the parties begin working together on developing a new story about what has happened, a story from which they can build a more promising future. "Perhaps our disagreement was unavoidable, but now that we see that, I wonder if we can put history behind us…"

---

53. Winslade, J. & Monk, G. (2000) *Narrative mediation: A new approach to conflict resolution.* San Francisco: Jossey-Bass.

Other practices for co-creating new realities include:

· Inviting participants to speak about what they value in the other. This is especially useful in breaking the tendency to cast the opposition as "all bad." This novel activity can also dislodge the scenario of mutual blame.

· Telling a story about when things went well together...

· Imagining the future in which the conflict had disappeared; describe it in detail, and discuss means of achieving this outcome together.

Creating Consciousness of Commonality: *"We are in this together."* Closely related to practices of creating new realities is the accentuation of commonality. If conflict is traditionally understood in terms of antagonists, one route to peace is to make visible the ways in which the parties are not antagonistic. Even more effective is to foreground the values or goals that unite them. Thus, government leaders often try to unite a nation steeped in internal conflict by locating an external threat. In the same way, police are cautioned in their attempts to quell domestic disputes, because marital partners screaming at each other may join in directing their abuse at the interfering officer. Of course, reducing conflict by finding a common enemy is scarcely ideal: it simply shifts the site of conflict. Among the more promising innovations for emphasizing commonality are:

· Generating discussion of common goals and how they might be served. Such discussion can be especially useful if such goals can only be reached by resolving the present conflict.

· Exploring together times in which each has faced difficult conditions that the other has also experienced.

· Inviting antagonists to speak about doubts they have in their position and/or the merits they find in the other's position. In both cases, their utterances will bring to light their areas of agreement.

· Open discussion with a period of silence, bringing into consciousness a sense of spiritual connection, a oneness.

· Working together on something commonly valued.

Becoming the Other: *"You and I are one."* A final logic for restoring peace relies on the traditional practice of sharing narratives, or more simply, telling stories to each other. Importantly, as one listens to stories, there is a common tendency to imagine oneself as the protagonist. One may privately experience oneself as the hero, the lover, the detective, the orphan, and so on. It is this very tendency that lends drama to stories: "I am in danger!" And when we listen to a friend tell of an adventure, we are begin to "feel with," or in a sense, to "become the friend." There are important implications here for peacebuilding. With careful forethought, conditions may be arranged so that either one or both antagonists may share their personal experiences relevant to the conflict. One may reveal the suffering of "what has it been like for me…" as a refugee, transgender person, a rape victim, a target of bullying, and so on. The listener may thus imagine oneself into the circumstances of the other, to "walk in his shoes," as it is said.

Practices of restorative justice rely heavily on such personal narratives. A more pointed use is made in practices of *outsider witnessing,* a significant advance in the use of story-telling.[54] Here an interviewer invites an offended individual into telling the personal

---

54. Carey, M. & Russell, S. (2003) Outsider-witness practices: Some answers to commonly asked questions. *International Journal of Narrative Therapy and Community Work.* 3-16

story in the presence of the antagonist or witness. For example, the story might focus on how the antagonist's actions have brought about long-term suffering for him and his family. The interviewer then asks the witness to re-tell what has been heard, possibly emphasizing elements in the story that seemed most important and that provided insight into the other's life. In this exchange, the witness does more than listen to the story; in the retelling he or she "becomes the other." Further, the offended individual now sees his or her story absorbed by the other. The process can also be extended, so the offended individual comments on the witnesses' re-telling and the insights of the witness could offer for them for their future. This kind of reciprocal witnessing contributes to mutual understanding and more productive dialogue.[55]

These five logics have figured in many innovative practices for relationally sensitive peace building. None of the practices should be considered out of historical or cultural context. Some may also be used in combination with others, but how they fit in the relational flow requires close attention to time and circumstance. This is also to encourage further innovation and sharing. As cultural conditions shift with time, so is there need for continuous creativity. The chief message in all of this is the pivotal significance of the *form of relational process* in reducing, resolving, or dissolving conflict.

---

55. Tochluk, S. (2010) *Witnessing whiteness: The need to talk about race and how to do it.* 2nd ed. R&L Education.

Toward Relational Governance

Processes of peacebuilding demand continuing attention. This is especially so in terms of the increasingly complex and consequential challenge of *governance* – that is, the process of ensuring the continuation of an acceptable form of collective life. In the present context, we may see this as sustaining a condition of relational coordination. To open discussion, consider a newly wedded couple struggling with the details of generating a harmonious way of living together. Who will do the cooking, cleaning, and pay the bills? How will they spend their evenings and weekends? Small questions, but their happiness depends on their coming into a condition of satisfactory coordination. Theorists often refer to this process as *self-organizing*, a term that may be applied in contexts ranging from two people to the totality of the earth's peoples.

As coordination is achieved, so does an acceptable or valued "way of life" begin to emerge. The challenge of governance is essentially that of sustaining this way of life. Thus, if the newly-weds successfully self-organize, how will they sustain their preferred way of life when in-laws visit, work-life becomes stressful, new friendships are formed, and so on. Will they use irritation and blame, argue, establish rules…? These are essentially practices of governance. In communities, informal process such as gossip and exclusion may be used to keep order; more formally, ordinances and police surveillance may do so. When an institution is established to ensure the valued patterns of relating are protected and sustained, we can speak of governments – from local and regional levels to the national and international.

The significant question is the process by which such institutions govern. Like newlyweds and communities, how do governments maintain order? This may be easy enough when there is broad and stable agreement on "the good way of life." Under these conditions, one might agree that "the less government the better." However, return here to the earlier discussion of multiple orderings and the emergence of conflict. When a community is composed of multiple enclaves – ethnic, religious, economic and so on – each with its preferred ways of living, governance becomes difficult. And when the conditions of life are continuously changing – economic, environmental, technological, and more – the complexities are compounded. Now consider our continuing concern in this book with rapid, unpredictable, and multiply repercussive change. Opinions and values forming and reforming, rights and duties everywhere in contention, opportunities emerging and disappearing, new flows of people and information…Are governments adequate to such challenges? Social unrest, angry protest, and insurrection are common fare in today's world. And if our existing institutions are inadequate, what does this mean for survival on the global level?

Government: Divided We Fall

There are longstanding critiques of all forms of government – Democracy, Autocracy, Oligarchy, Totalitarianism, etc. As Winston Churchill once remarked, "Democracy is the worst form of government, except for all those other forms that have been tried." Here it is important to realize that when we understand government as an established entity with specific responsibilities we are once again assuming a world of separations. Thus, we presume that governments are more or less *bounded entities*, with an inside and an outside. *We,* the citizens, are the outsiders, and *they,* the decision makers, are inside. The doors may be opened to us or closed, at the will of the governing body. Echoing our discussion in Chapter 1, we thus confront an array of unfortunate outcomes. For example, as bounded entities governments tend to:

- *Develop "insider" realities and logics* that may be cut away from the public outside. The inside view of "what's good for society" may not agree with vast sectors of the public.

- *Create public suspicion* about the motives and rationality of their decisions. There will be many outside who find the decision or policy foolish, limited, inhumane, or self-serving. Encouraged in the population is thus a sense that "it's us against them."

- *Embrace a cause-and-effect orientation* to policymaking, in which "we," the governing body, cause "them," the public, to act as we see best. This orientation, often called *governmentality*, functions impersonally and insensitively.[56] It dehumanizes the people by treating them as objects to be shaped and controlled. The result is often public irritation and resistance, or docile passivity.

- *Promote their own strength and power*. Those within the government often seek means of sustaining or expanding their positions of power. In effect, they are self-interested, while investments in the public good become secondary.

Most readers can quickly identify such outcomes in their own lives. The problems are intensified when there are competing politi-

---

56. Rose, N., O'Malley, P. & Valverde, M. (2009) Governmentality. *Annual Review of Law and Social Science*. 2, 83-104.

cal parties, each seeking dominance. Careful deliberation on complex policy issues will be replaced by one-sided argument, in which the realities and logic of one side will be systematically scorned by the other. Again, concern with the public good is sacrificed. It is "what's good for the party" that counts, and not "what's good for the people." Additional difficulties stem from the voting process itself, as it encourages individuals to think primarily of "what *I* want" as opposed to the public good.

When we turn to global governance, we realize the imperative need for innovation. The demands for international collaboration have never been greater. We confront globe-spanning problems of economy, health, justice, the environment, and more. All these issues are related; all have life-threatening consequences. And yet, in our efforts to deal with these challenges, we primarily rely on a conception of *independent* governments. And it is this assumption of separation that invites each nation state to be chiefly invested in its own wellbeing. Thus, despite world wars, atomic threats, sweeping viruses, and environmental decay, the nations of the world remain distrustful of each other, locked in competition and unceasing conflict. Planetary survival is in jeopardy.

Vistas in Relational Governance

Here we enter new and relatively unexplored territory: *relational governance*. What would it mean for the practice of governing if we approached from a relational standpoint? This is not an idle question, especially in the context of increasing political polarization, mass civil unrest, police violence, and military intervention in public life. As well, digital technology and social media enable grassroots organizations to rapidly spring to life, each with its own values and vision of the world. Impassioned movements incite and intensify social conflicts and destabilize governments.

Importantly, these conditions of agitation have also given rise to widespread curiosity and creativity. We find increasing attempts to explore how governance could be otherwise. Most fascinating is the family resemblance characterizing a broad array of movements and social experiments from all corners of the world. Consider, for example, movements in co-governance, collaborative governance, New Public Governance, participatory governance, the people's parliament, the relational state, and more.[57] Among their prominent features are:

- *Inclusive participation*. A major concern is the growing sense of frustration among citizens that they have no voice in the decisions that shape their future. Effective means are sought for expanding the active participation of people in political decision-making. In these attempts the separation of *the* government from *the* people is lessened.

- *Decentralized decision making*. Given the enormous complexity and conditions of rapid change, "policies for all" approximate "policies for no one." Because top-down decisions increasingly meet with resistance, their efficacy is undermined. A premium is thus placed on more localized or context-sensitive decision making.

- *Productive dialogue*. A strong emphasis is placed on dialogic practice as a major vehicle for enhancing governance. However, because conversations can also be contentious and polarizing, forms of generative dialogue are pursued.

---

57. Additional movements include commons-based decision making, the cooperative movement, deliberative democracy, dialogic policymaking, participatory democracy, the people's assembly, relational welfare, and the relational state.

· *Collaboration.* There is consistent recognition that collaboration among people and institutions is essential to our future well-being.

To conclude, there is inspiration to be found in several illustrations of these movements in action. On the local level, activists in many countries are concerned that the public services provided by national and state governments don't meet the needs of the people. For example, services in health care, unemployment, housing, and elder care are often underfunded, inflexible, and burdened by bureaucracy. Significant movements in Denmark and the UK demonstrate the potentials of community organizing for filling the gap. Rather than waiting passively and resentfully for services, the attempt is to generate relationships within the community through which they can achieve what the government cannot. Thus, in the UK activists have generated community meetings in which inhabitants share experiences, knowledge, and wisdom. From these, networks could be developed that enabled community members to help each other find meaningful work, support their health, and provide services for the elderly.[58] Moving a step further, public welfare agencies in a Danish city joined together in actively seeking community collaboration in providing services. This was especially important in neighborhoods where immigrant populations were both needy and lacking knowledge of available supports. By working with the people, the government services could be more finely tuned to the context of need.[59]

---

58. Cottam, H. (2018) *Radical help: How we can remake the relationships among us and revolutionize the welfare state.* London: Virago.

59. Von Heimburg, D., Ness, O. & Storch, J. (2021) Co-creation of public values: Citizenship, social justice, and well-being. In A.O. Thomassen & J.B Jensen (Eds.) *Processual perspectives on the co-productive turn in public sector organizations.* Hershey, PA: IGI Global

Moving to the regional level, an important challenge in the Northeast coast of the U.S has been the dramatic decline in the population of fish. Replenishment has become an urgent need. A collaborative effort was thus designed in which agencies from the national government, the state government, Indian tribes with fishing rights, non-government organizations, scientists, and citizens all participated. The case is especially interesting, as it illustrates the complexities of multi-party collaboration.[60] Agreeing to work together toward a common goal was only the first step toward productive coordination. A second challenge was in organizing the process. Questions concerning respective rights and duties, leadership, and decision rules also had to be worked out. Answers to these questions required years of experimentation and adjustment. A third challenge to productive coordination lay in the process of communication itself. Coming from different backgrounds, perspectives, positions of authority, and values, the micro process of relating was not easy. When we are all trained in different dances, how can we dance together? Relational governance is not an effortless achievement, but this collaboration did make a significant difference to the environment.

Coda

Wherever people can mingle, so can they create centers of meaning and value, mini forms of life with their own trajectories and innovations. The current and coming technologies of relating dramatically increase the opportunities for such mingling – globally

---

60. In Emerson, K. and Nabatchi, T. (2015) *Collaborative governance regimes*. Washington DC: Georgetown University Press.

and instantaneously. We thus approach a global condition in which the traditional means for structuring our lives will lose their ordering capacities. The influence of family traditions, schools, law enforcement agencies, corporations, religions, and governments will give way to the mammoth force of uncontrollable co-creation. One could see this as a new world of radical liberation, in which the full potentials of humankind may be opened for exploration. Conversely, with each form of life seeking its own precious ends, we approach a full-scale Armageddon of all against all. If we continue our focus on the welfare of bounded units – individual persons, families, communities, governments, religions, and so on – we will invite just such a war. As proposed in the present work, our hope lies in placing processes of relating at the center of our attention, caring for and creating practices that enable us to live and thrive together. It is my deepest hope that the pages of this book have offered resources for the rigorous travels ahead.

Further Resources

Coleman, P.T., Deutsch, M., & Marcus, E.C. (Eds.) (2014) *The handbook of conflict resolution: Theory and practice.* 3rd.ed. San Francisco: Jossey Bass.

Cottam, H. (2018) *Radical help: How we can remake the relationships among us and revolutionize the welfare state.* London: Virago.

Crosby, B.C. & Bryson, J.M. (2005) *Leadership for the common good: Tackling problems in a shared-power world.* San Francisco: Jossey Bass 2nd ed.

Emerson, K. & Nabatchi, T. (2015) *Collaborative governance regimes,* Georgetown University Press.

Flaskas, C., McCarthy, I., & Sheehan, J. (Eds.) (2007). *Hope and despair in narrative and family therapy: Adversity, forgiveness, and reconciliation.* London: Routledge.

Hassan, Z. (2014) *The social labs revolution: A new approach to solving our most complex challenges.* San Francisco: Barrett-Koehler.

Sampson, C. (2010). *Positive approaches to peacebuilding: A resource for innovators.* Chagrin Falls, OH: Taos Institute.

Schoem, D. & Hurtado, S. (Eds.) (2004). *Intergroup dialogue: Deliberative democracy in school, college, community, and workplace.* Ann Harbor: The University of Michigan Press.

Sorensen, E. & Torfing, J. (Eds.) (2016) *Theories of democratic network governance.* London: Palgrave

Stearns, P. (Eds.) (2018). *Peacebuilding through dialogue: Education, human transformation, and conflict resolution.* Fairfax: George Mason University Press.

Toulouse, P. R. (2018) *Truth and reconciliation in Canadian schools.* Winnipeg: Portage and Main Press.

Taos Institute Publications Books in Print

Taos Tempo Series: Collaborative Practices for Changing Times

Thriving Women, Thriving World: An Invitation to Dialogue, Healing and Inspired Actions (2019) by Diana Whitney, Caroline Adams Miller, Tanya Cruz Teller, Marlene Ogawa, Jessica Cocciolone, Haesun Moon, Kathryn Britton, Angela Koh & Alejandra Leon de la Barra (also available as an e-book)

Paths to Positive Aging: Dog Days with a Bone and other Essays, (2017) by Kenneth J. Gergen and Mary Gergen

The Magic of Organizational Life, (2017) by Mette Larsen

70Candles! Women Thriving in their 8th Decade, (2015) by Jane Giddan and Ellen Cole (also available as an e-book)

Social Constructionist Perspectives on Group Work, (2015) by Emerson F. Rasera, Editor

U & Me: Communicating in Moments that Matter, (Revised edition 2014) by John Steward (also available as an e-book)

Relational Leading: Practices for Dialogically Based Collaborations, (2013) by Lone Hersted and Ken Gergen (also available as an e-book)

Retiring but Not Shy: Feminist Psychologists Create their Post-Careers, (2012) by Ellen Cole and Mary Gergen. (also available as an e-book)

Developing Relational Leadership: Resources for Developing Reflexive Organizational Practices, (2012) by Carsten Hornstrup, Jesper Loehr-Petersen, Joergen Gjengedal Madsen, Thomas Johansen, Allan Vinther Jensen (also available as an e-book)

Practicing Relational Ethics in Organizations, (2012) by Gitte Haslebo and Maja Loua Haslebo

Healing Conversations Now: Enhance Relationships with Elders and Dying Loved Ones, (2011) by Joan Chadbourne and Tony Silbert

Riding the Current: How to Deal with the Daily Deluge of Data, (2010) by Madelyn Blair

Ordinary Life Therapy: Experiences from a Collaborative Systemic Practice, (2009) by Carina Håkansson

Mapping Dialogue: Essential Tools for Social Change, (2008) by Marianne "Mille" Bojer, Heiko Roehl, Mariane Knuth-Hollesen, and Colleen Magner

Positive Family Dynamics: Appreciative Inquiry Questions to Bring Out the Best in Families, (2008) by Dawn Cooperrider Dole, Jen Hetzel Silbert, Ada Jo Mann, and Diana Whitney

****

Focus Book Series

The Relational Imperative: Resources for a World on Edge, (2021) by Kenneth J. Gergen

Dialogic Social Inquiry: Qualitative Research without a Methodological Map, (2021) by Jan N. DeFehr, Cynthia Loreto Sosa Infante, & Christian Israel Lizama Valladares

STAN and The Four Fantastic Powers: The First Appreciative Inquiry Book for Kids, (2018) by Shira Levy, Marge Schiller, Sarah Schiller, Max Schiller, and illustrator, Stephanie Rudolph

Coordinated Management of Meaning, CMM: A Research Manual, (2017) by Natalie Rascon and Stephen Littlejohn (also available as an e-book)

Communicating Possibilities: A Brief Introduction to the Coordinated Management of Meaning (CMM), (2017) by Ilene C. Wasserman and Beth Fisher-Yoshida (also available as an e-book)

A Student's Guide to Clinical Supervision, (2014) by Glenn E. Boyd

When Stories Clash: Addressing Conflict with Narrative Mediation, (2013) by Gerald Monk and John Winslade (also available as an e-book)

Bereavement Support Groups: Breathing Life Into Stories of the Dead (2012) by Lorraine Hedtke (also available as an e-book)

The Appreciative Organization, (Revised edition 2008) by Harlene Anderson, David Cooperrider, Ken Gergen, Mary Gergen, Sheila McNamee, Jane Watkins, and Diana Whitney

Appreciative Inquiry: A Positive Approach to Building Cooperative Capacity, (2005) by Frank Barrett and Ronald Fry (also available as an e-book)

Dynamic Relationships: Unleashing the Power of Appreciative Inquiry in Daily Living, (2005) by Jacqueline Stavros and Cheri B. Torres

Appreciative Sharing of Knowledge: Leveraging Knowledge Management for Strategic Change, (2004) by Tojo Thatchenkery

Social Construction: Entering the Dialogue, (2004) by Kenneth J. Gergen, and Mary Gergen (also available as an e-book)

Appreciative Leaders: In the Eye of the Beholder, (2001) edited by Marge Schiller, Bea Mah Holland, and Deanna Riley

Experience AI: A Practitioner's Guide to Integrating Appreciative Inquiry and Experiential Learning, (2001) by Miriam Ricketts and Jim Willis

****

Books for Professionals Series

Appreciative Inquiry as a Daily Leadership Practice: Realizing Change One Conversation at a Time, (2020) by Luc Verheijen, Saskia Tjepkema, Joeri Kabalt

Social Constructionist Perspectives on Group Work, (2015) by Emerson F. Rasera, Editor

New Horizons in Buddhist Psychology: Relational Buddhism for Collaborative Practitioners, (2010) edited by Maurits G.T. Kwee

Positive Approaches to Peacebuilding: A Resource for Innovators, (2010) edited by Cynthia Sampson, Mohammed Abu-Nimer, Claudia Liebler, and Diana Whitney

Social Construction on the Edge: 'Withness'-Thinking & Embodiment, (2010) by John Shotter

Joined Imagination: Writing and Language in Therapy, (2009) by Peggy Penn

Celebrating the Other: A Dialogic Account of Human Nature, (reprint 2008) by Edward Sampson

Conversational Realities Revisited: Life, Language, Body and World, (2008) by John Shotter

Horizons in Buddhist Psychology: Practice, Research and Theory (2006) edited by Maurits Kwee, Kenneth J. Gergen, and Fusako Koshikawa

Therapeutic Realities: Collaboration, Oppression and Relational Flow, (2005) by Kenneth J. Gergen

SocioDynamic Counselling: A Practical Guide to Meaning Making, (2004) by R. Vance Peavy

Experiential Exercises in Social Construction – A Fieldbook for Creating Change, (2004) by Robert Cottor, Alan Asher, Judith Levin, and Cindy Weiser

Dialogues About a New Psychology, (2004) by Jan Smedslund

****

WorldShare Books – Free PDF Download

*Re-Sounding: Introducing an alternative metaphor for organization change (*PDF version 2021) by Rik Spann and Simon Martin

Construção Social em Ação:Contribuições da Conferência de 25 anos de Aniversário do Taos Institute Organização da Versão em Português, (PDF version 2021), tradutoras: Carla Guanaes-Lorenzi, Domitila Shizue Kawakami Gonzaga & Giovanna Cabral Coricci

Palabras, Movimientos y Emociones: Nuestro homenaje a Tom Andersen, (PDF version 2020), Editoras: Adela G. García y Leticia G. Rodriguez, Editora invitada: Helena Maffei Cruz, Consejo Latino Americano del Taos Institute, TILAC

Social Construction in Action: The Taos Institute's Silver Jubilee, (PDF version 2020), edited by Alexandra Arnold, Kristin Bodiford, Pamela Brett-MacLean, Dawn Dole, Angela Maria Estrada, Fran Lyon Dugin, Bonnie Milne, W. Ellen Raboin, Paloma Torres-Dávila, and Carlos Felipe Villar-Guhl

Rhetoric in Action, Philosophy, Psychology, and Politics, (PDF version 2020), by Herbert W. Simons

Terapia Colaborativa: Relaciones y Conversaciones Que Hacen Una Diferencia, (PDF version 2020), Adela Garcia, Editor

Harlene, conversaciones interrumpidas, (PDF version 2019), by Harlene Anderson, Rocío Chaveste y ML Papusa Molina, compiladoras

Cultural Dialogue at Home – Austrian Hosts and Syrian Refugees: An Autoethnographic Narrative, (PDF version 2019) By Corina Ahlers

A Systemic Community: Collaborative Leadership, Redescription and Evolutionary Ways of Becoming, (PDF version 2019), by Jacob Storch

Social Texts and Context: Literature and Social Psychology, (PDF version 2018), by Jonathan Potter, Peter Stringer, Margaret Wetherell

Lifescaping Project: Action Research and Appreciative Inquiry in San Francisco Bay Area Schools, (PDF version 2017), edited by Rolla E. Lewis, Ardella Dailey, Greg Jennings, Peg Windelman

Disarmed Warriors: Narratives with Youth Ex-Combatants in Colombia, (PDF version 2017), by Victoria Lugo

Spirituality, Social Construction and Relational Processes: Essays and Reflections, (PDF version 2016) edited by Duane Bidwell

Therapy as a Hermeneutic and Constructionist Dialogue: Practices of freedom and of deco-construction in the relational, language and meaning games, (PDF version 2016) by Gilberto Limon (Translated from Spanish)

Recovered Without Treatment: The Process of Abandoning Crystal Meth Use Without Professional Help, (PDF version 2016) by Pavel Nepustil

Introduction to Group Dynamics: Social Construction Approach to Organizational Development and Community Revitalization, (PDF version 2016), by Toshio Sugiman

Recursos psico-sociales para el post-conflicto" (Psico-social resources for post-conflict), (PDF version 2016), edited by Angela Maria Estrada

Buddha As Therapist: Meditations, (PDF version 2015), by G.T. Maurits Kwee

Diálogos para la transformación: experiencias en terapia y Otras intervenciones psicosociales en Iberoamérica – Volumen 1 and 2, (PDF version 2015), by Dora Fried Schnitman, Editora

Education as Social Construction: Contributions to Theory, Research and Practice, (PDF version 2015) Editors: Thalia Dragonas, Kenneth J. Gergen, Sheila McNamee, Eleftheria Tseliou

Psychosocial Innovation in Post-War Sri Lanka, (PDF version 2015) by Laurie Charles and Gameela Samarasinghe

Social Accountability & Selfhood, (PDF version 2015, original publication date – 1984, Basil Blackwell, Inc.) by John Shotter

Construccionismo Social Y Discusion De Paradrigmas En Psycologia: Indeterminacion, Holismo y Juegos de Lenguaje vs. La Teoria Pictorica del Lenguaje, (PDF versión 2015) by Roberto Aristequi

{In}Credible Leadership: A Guide for Shared Understanding and Application, (PDF version 2015) by Yuzanne Mare, Isabel Meyer, Elonya Niehaus-Coetzee, Johann Roux

Etnia Terapéutica: Integrando Entornos, (PDF version 2015) by Jeannette Samper A. and José Antonio Garciandía I

Post-modern Education & Development, (Chinese edition, PDF version 2014) Introduction by Shi-Jiuan Wu (後現代教育與發展　介紹 吳熙琄)

Exceeding Expectations: An Anthology of Appreciative Inquiry Stories in Education from Around the World, (PDF version 2014), Story Curators: Dawn Dole, Matthew Moehle, and Lindsey Godwin

The Discursive Turn in Social Psychology, (PDF version 2014), by Nikos Bozatzis & Thalia Dragonas (Eds.)

New Paradigms, Culture and Subjectivity, (PDF version 2014), edited by Dora Fried Schnitman and Jorge Schnitman

Happily Different: Sustainable Educational Change – A Relational Approach, (PDF version 2014), by Loek Schoenmakers

Strategising through Organising: The Significance of Relational Sensemaking, (PDF version 2013), by Mette Vinther Larsen

Therapists in Continuous Education: A Collaborative Approach, (PDF version 2013), by Ottar Ness

Contextualizing Care: Relational Engagement with/in Human Service Practices, (PDF version 2013), by Janet Newbury

Nuevos Paradigmas, Cultura y Subjetividad, (PDF versión 2017) by Dora Fried Schnitman

Novos Paradigmas Em Mediação, (PDF versión, original publicación date 1999). Dora Fried Schnitman y Stephen LittleJohn (Editors)

Filo y Sofía En Diálogo: La poesía social de la conversación terapéutica, (PDF versión 2013, original publicación date 2000), Klaus G. Deissler y Sheila McNamee (editors). Traducción al español: Mario O. Castillo Rangel

Socially Constructing God: Evangelical Discourse on Gender and the Divine, (PDF version 2013), by Landon P. Schnabel

Ohana and the Creation of a Therapeutic Community, (PDF version 2013), by Celia Studart Quintas

From Nonsense Syllables to Holding Hands: Sixty Years as a Psychologist, (PDF version 2013), by Jan Smedslund

Management and Organization: Relational Alternatives to Individualism, (PDF version 2013), reprinted with permission. Edited by Dian Marie Hosking, H. Peter Dachler, Kenneth J. Gergen

Appreciative Inquiry to Promote Local Innovations among Farmers Adapting to Climate Change, (PDF version 2013) by Shayamal Saha

La terapia Multi–Being. Una prospettiva relazionale in psicoterapia, (PDF versión 2013) by Diego Romaioli

Psychotherapy by Karma Transformation: Relational Buddhism and Rational Practice, (PDF version 2013) by G.T. Maurits Kwee

La terapia como diálogo hermenéutico y construccionista: Márgenes de libertad y deco-construcción en los juegos relacionales, de lenguaje y de significado, (PDF versión 2012) by Gilberto Limón Arce

Wittgenstein in Practice: His Philosophy of Beginnings, and Beginnings, and Beginnings, (PDF version 2012) by John Shotter

Social Construction of the Person, (PDF version 2012). Editors: Kenneth J. Gergen and Keith M. Davis, Original copyright date: 1985, Springer-Verlag, New York, Inc.

Images of Man, (PDF version 2012) by John Shotter. Original copyright date: 1975, Methuen, London

Ethical Ways of Being, (PDF version 2012) by Dirk Kotze, Johan Myburg, Johann Roux, and Associates. Original copyright date: 2002, Ethics Alive, Institute for Telling Development, Pretoria, South Africa

Piemp, (PDF version 2012) by Theresa Hulme. Published in Afrikaans

For book information and ordering, visit Taos Institute Publications at:
www.taosinstitutepublications.net

For further information, call: 1-440-338-6733
Email: info@taosinstitute.net

www.ingramcontent.com/pod-product-compliance
Lightning Source LLC
Chambersburg PA
CBHW051716090426
42738CB00010B/1932